P9-CBB-615

# A CENTURY OF "BANDE DESSINEE"

Beginning with the raucous *Pieds Nickelés* comic strip created in 1908 by the French cartoonist Louis Forton, French-language comics have brought laughter and thrills to millions upon millions of kids for just over a century now.

*La bande dessinée*, as they call it, found its uncontested master in 1929 when a young Belgian cartoonist named Georges Remi, inspired by Alain St.-Ogan's popular *Zig et Puce* comic strip (itself in turn inspired by 1920s American comic strips), produced the first installments of *Tintin* for *Le Petit XXe*. Thanks to the oddly-coiffed young reporter and his dog Snowy, the man who signed his work Hergé became, within a decade, the most popular cartoonist in Europe (and has remained so ever since).

The 25 years after World War II, from 1945 to 1970, were a true golden age for Franco-Belgian comics, published in hugely popular weekly magazines as *Spirou*, *Tintin*, and *Pilote*. Standout cartoonists included André Franquin (*Spirou*, *Gaston Lagaffe*), Fred (*Philémon*), Jean Giraud (*Blueberry*), E.P. Jacobs (*Blake and Mortimer*), Raymond Macherot (*Chlorophylle and Sibylline*), Jacques Martin (*Alix*), Jean-Claude Mézières (*Valérian*), Morris (*Lucky Luke*), Peyo (*The Smurfs*), Maurice Tillieux (*Gil Jourdan*), Will (*Tif et Tondu*), and Hergé's only true rival, the René Goscinny/Albert Uderzo team behind the monster hit *Astérix*. And while that golden age is now a receding dot in our rear-view mirror, to this day marvelous new work continues to be created and released by cartoonists young and old.

Many of these great comics have been released in English-language editions by such publishers as NBM, Cinebook, and Little, Brown and Company — but others remain elusive, buried treasures to the American public. We here at Fantagraphics have brought out our finest picks and shovels to unearth some of our favorites.

Our journey into the world of the *la bande dessinée* began with two recent masterpieces by French cartoonists who usually create darker, more adult work: David B. (of *Epileptic* fame), who brought a classic story by the French novelist and songwriter Pierre Mac Orlan, *The Littlest Pirate King*, to sumptuous visual life — while the provocative underground cartoonist Stéphane Blanquet took us for a visit to the *Toys in the Basement*. This year we have gone back half a century to bring you two masterpieces from the pages of *Spirou* magazine, the aforementioned *Gil Jourdan* by Tillieux and *Sibylline* by Macherot, translated into English for the very first time. What will 2012 bring? *Qui sait?* ("Who knows?")

—Kim Thompson, editor

R. MACHEROT

# SiBYL-ANNE
# VS. RATTiCUS

FANTAGRAPHICS BOOKS

Edited and translated by Kim Thompson. Series design by Jacob Covey. Book design and lettering by Alexa Koenings. Production by Paul Baresh. Macherot fonts created by Alexa Koenings. Associate Editor: Eric Reynolds. Published by Gary Groth and Kim Thompson. Special thanks to Stephan Caluwaerts, André Taymans, and Jean Gaignade. *Sibyl-Anne vs. Ratticus (Sibylline en Danger*, originally serialized in *Spirou* magazine from #1488 to #1497 [1966] and from #1510 to #1529 [1967]) © 2011 Editions Flouzemaker — Belgium. This edition © 2011 Fantagraphics Books. All rights reserved, permission to quote or reproduce material for reviews or notices must be obtained from Fantagraphics Books, in writing, at 7563 Lake City Way NE, Seattle, WA 98115. Visit Fantagraphics online at www.fantagraphics.com. Distributed to bookstores in the U.S. by W.W. Norton and Company, Inc. (800-233-4830). Distributed to comics shops in the U.S. by Diamond Comic Distributors (800-452-6642 ex215). Distributed in Canada by Canadian Manda Group (800-452-6642 ex862). Distributed in the U.K. by Turnaround (20-8829-3002) First edition May, 2011. Printed in Singapore. ISBN 978-1-60699-452-8.

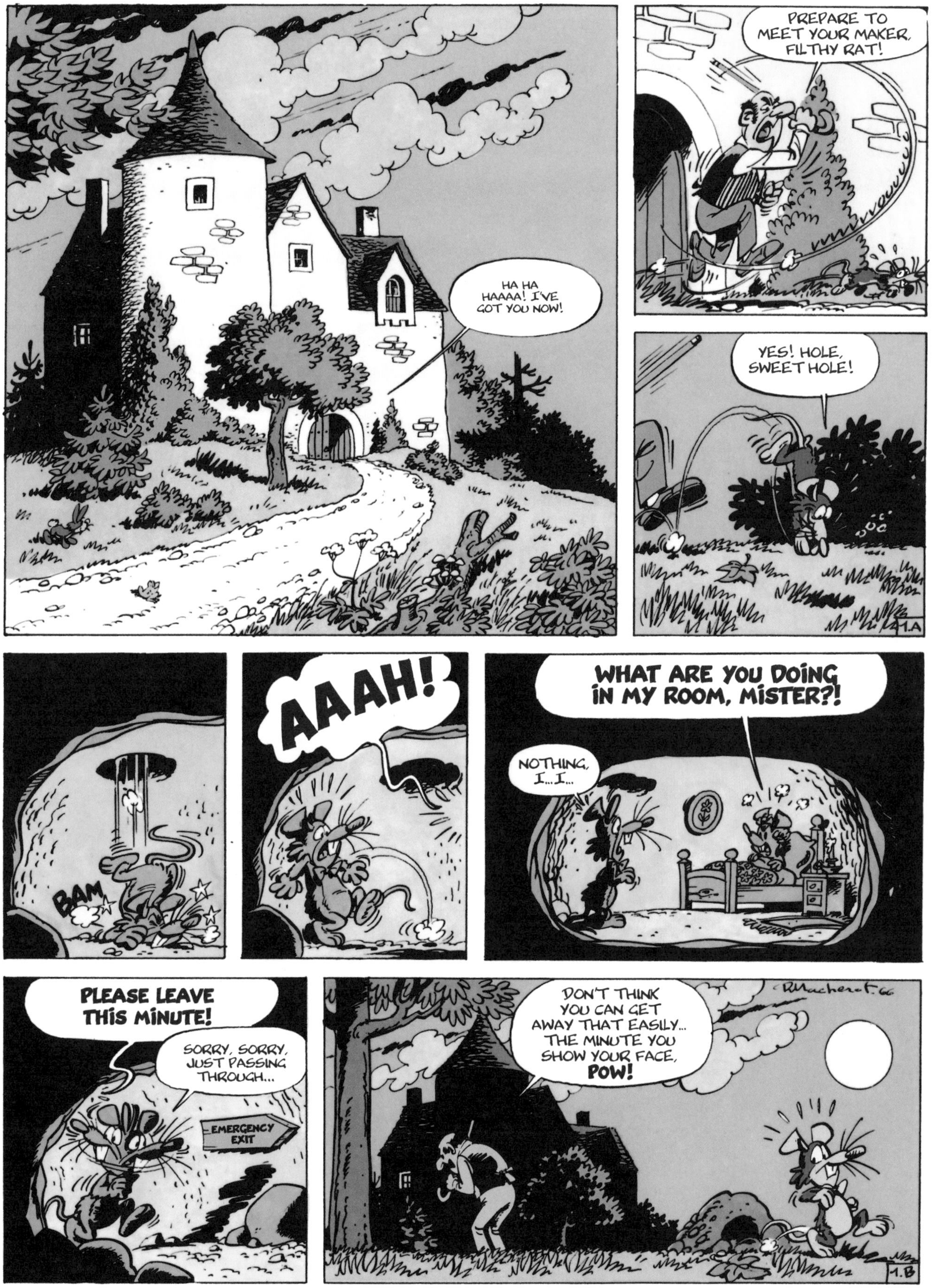
HA HA HAAAA! I'VE GOT YOU NOW!
PREPARE TO MEET YOUR MAKER, FILTHY RAT!
YES! HOLE, SWEET HOLE!
1.A
BAM
AAAH!
WHAT ARE YOU DOING IN MY ROOM, MISTER?!
NOTHING, I... I...
PLEASE LEAVE THIS MINUTE!
SORRY, SORRY, JUST PASSING THROUGH...
EMERGENCY EXIT
DON'T THINK YOU CAN GET AWAY THAT EASILY... THE MINUTE YOU SHOW YOUR FACE, POW!
1.B

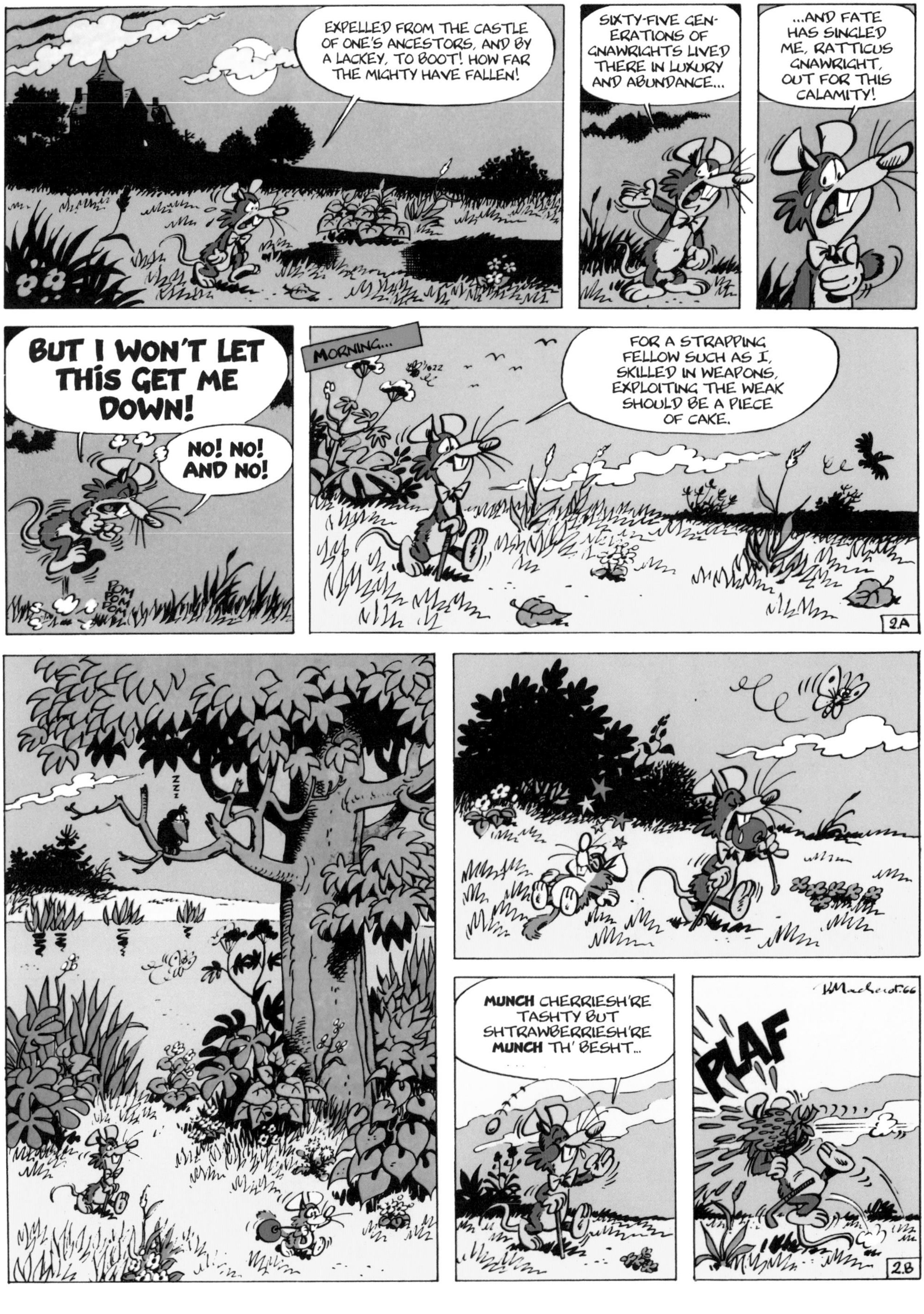
EXPELLED FROM THE CASTLE OF ONE'S ANCESTORS, AND BY A LACKEY, TO BOOT! HOW FAR THE MIGHTY HAVE FALLEN!
SIXTY-FIVE GENERATIONS OF GNAWRIGHTS LIVED THERE IN LUXURY AND ABUNDANCE...
...AND FATE HAS SINGLED ME, RATTICUS GNAWRIGHT, OUT FOR THIS CALAMITY!
BUT I WON'T LET THIS GET ME DOWN!
NO! NO! AND NO!
POM POM POM
MORNING...
FOR A STRAPPING FELLOW SUCH AS I, SKILLED IN WEAPONS, EXPLOITING THE WEAK SHOULD BE A PIECE OF CAKE.
2.A
MUNCH CHERRIESH'RE TASHTY BUT SHTRAWBERRIESH'RE MUNCH TH' BESHT...
PLAF
2.B

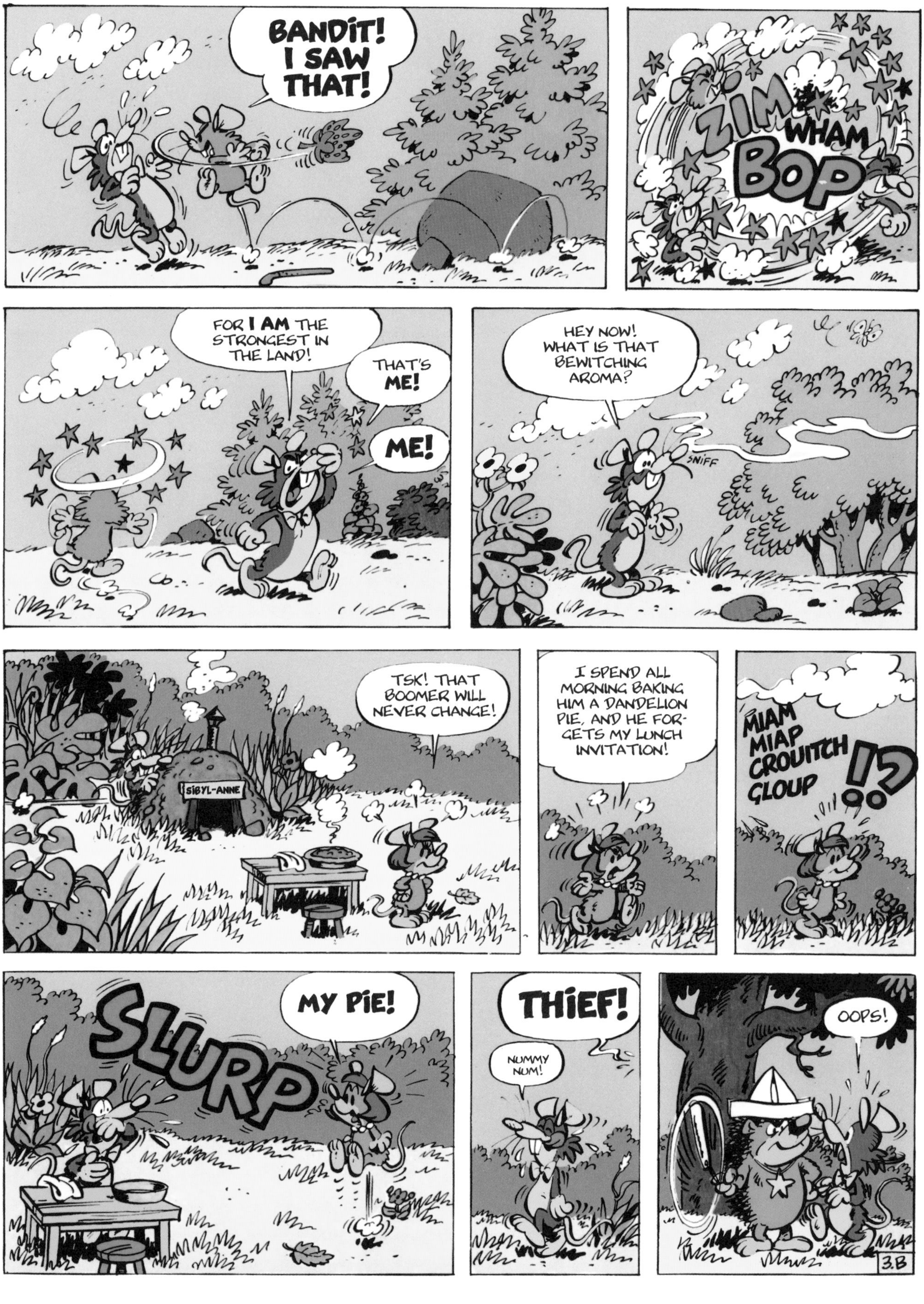
BANDIT! I SAW THAT!
ZIM WHAM BOP
FOR I AM THE STRONGEST IN THE LAND!
THAT'S ME!
ME!
HEY NOW! WHAT IS THAT BEWITCHING AROMA?
SNIFF
SIBYL-ANNE
TSK! THAT BOOMER WILL NEVER CHANGE!
I SPEND ALL MORNING BAKING HIM A DANDELION PIE, AND HE FORGETS MY LUNCH INVITATION!
MIAM MIAP CROUITCH GLOUP
!?
SLURP
MY PIE!
THIEF!
NUMMY NUM!
OOPS!
3.B

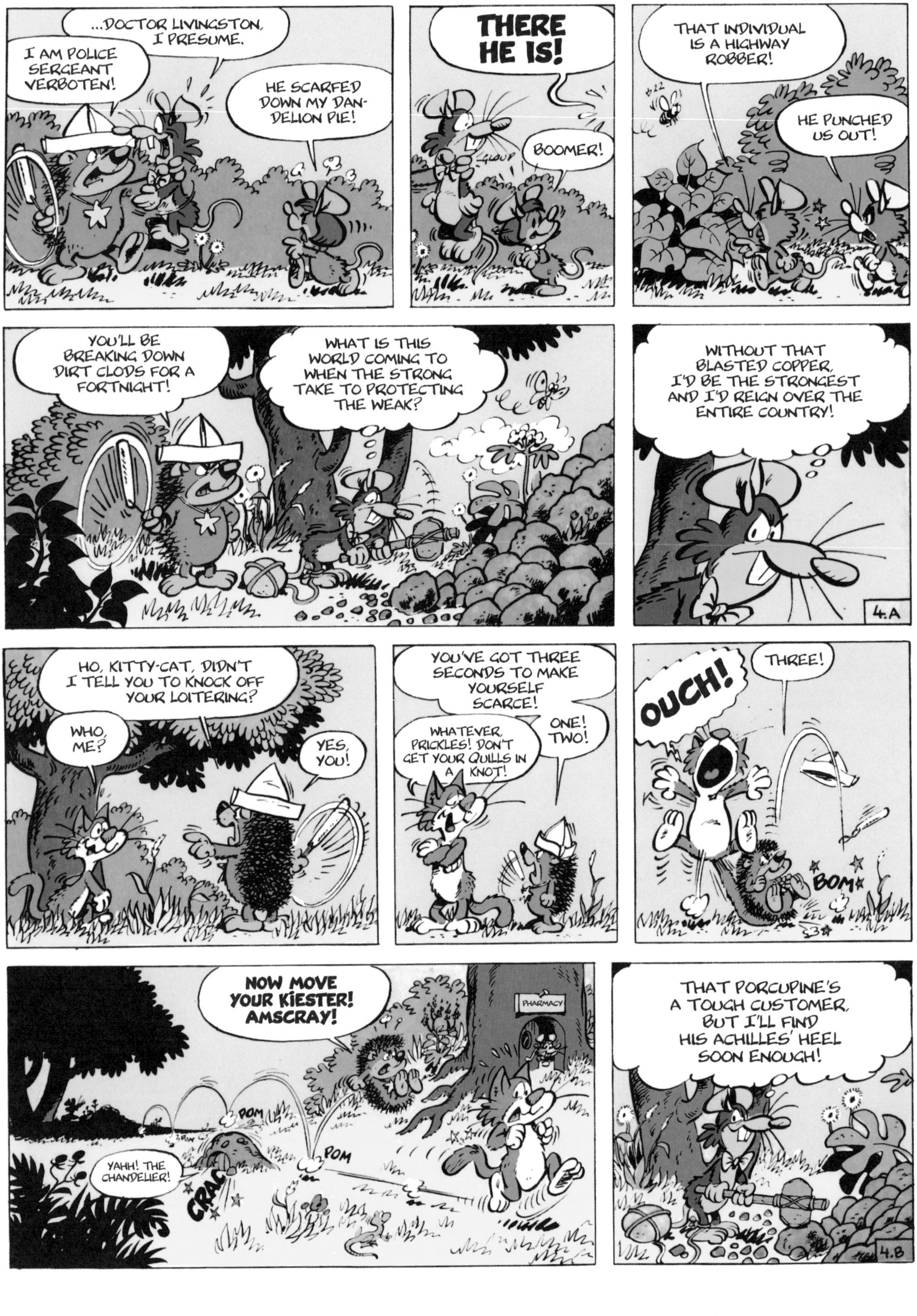
I AM POLICE SERGEANT VERBOTEN!
...DOCTOR LIVINGSTON, I PRESUME.
HE SCARFED DOWN MY DAN-DELION PIE!
THERE HE IS!
BOOMER!
THAT INDIVIDUAL IS A HIGHWAY ROBBER!
HE PUNCHED US OUT!
YOU'LL BE BREAKING DOWN DIRT CLODS FOR A FORTNIGHT!
WHAT IS THIS WORLD COMING TO WHEN THE STRONG TAKE TO PROTECTING THE WEAK?
WITHOUT THAT BLASTED COPPER, I'D BE THE STRONGEST AND I'D REIGN OVER THE ENTIRE COUNTRY!
4.A
HO, KITTY-CAT, DIDN'T I TELL YOU TO KNOCK OFF YOUR LOITERING?
WHO, ME?
YES, YOU!
YOU'VE GOT THREE SECONDS TO MAKE YOURSELF SCARCE!
WHATEVER, PRICKLES! DON'T GET YOUR QUILLS IN A KNOT!
ONE! TWO!
OUCH!
THREE!
BOM
NOW MOVE YOUR KIESTER! AMSCRAY!
PHARMACY
POM
POM
YAHH! THE CHANDELIER!
CRAC
THAT PORCUPINE'S A TOUGH CUSTOMER, BUT I'LL FIND HIS ACHILLES' HEEL SOON ENOUGH!
4.B

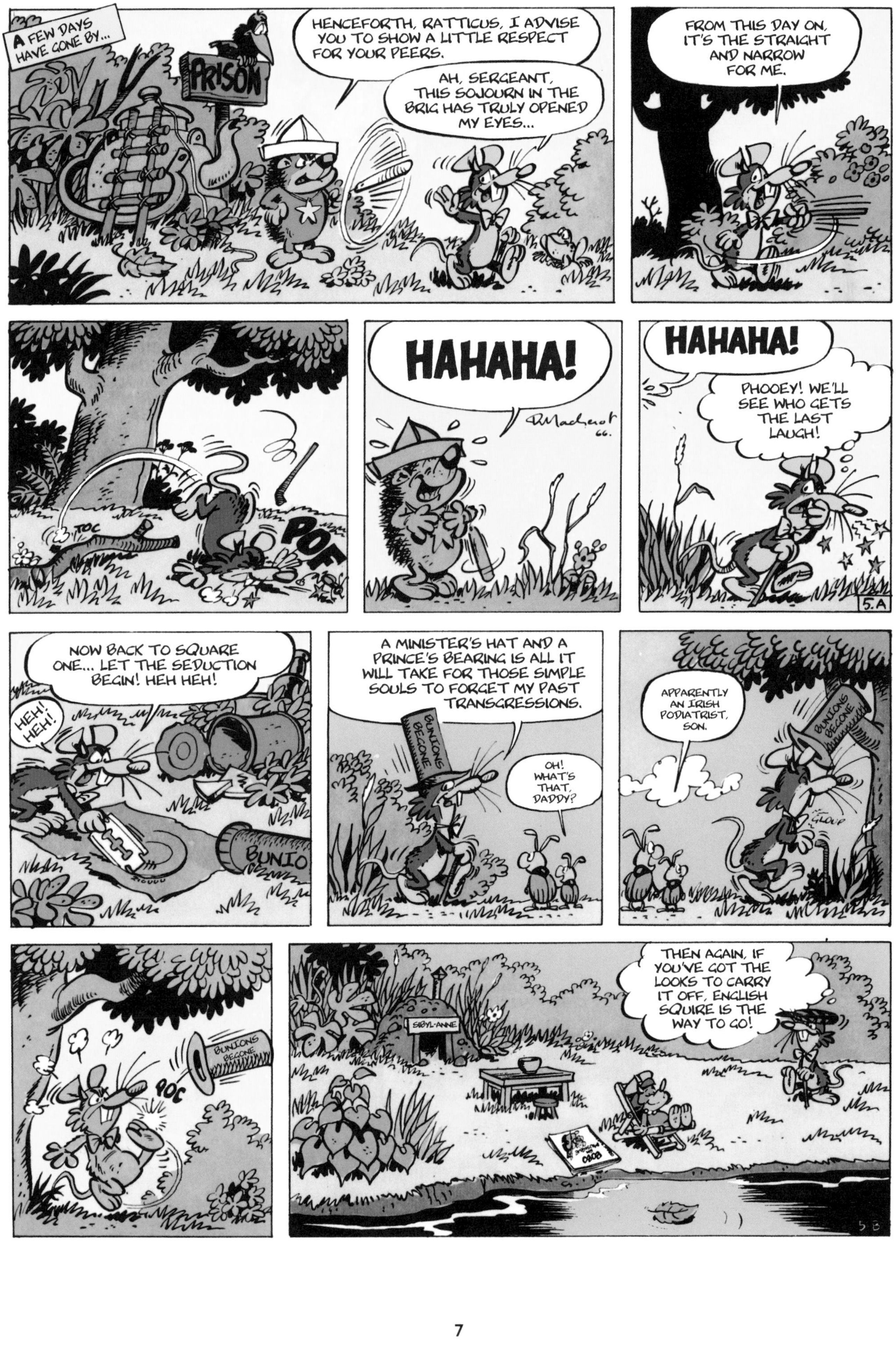
A FEW DAYS HAVE GONE BY...
PRISON
HENCEFORTH, RATTICUS, I ADVISE YOU TO SHOW A LITTLE RESPECT FOR YOUR PEERS.
AH, SERGEANT, THIS SOJOURN IN THE BRIG HAS TRULY OPENED MY EYES...
FROM THIS DAY ON, IT'S THE STRAIGHT AND NARROW FOR ME.
TOC
POF
HAHAHA!
HAHAHA!
PHOOEY! WE'LL SEE WHO GETS THE LAST LAUGH!
5.A
NOW BACK TO SQUARE ONE... LET THE SEDUCTION BEGIN! HEH HEH!
HEH! HEH!
BUNIO
A MINISTER'S HAT AND A PRINCE'S BEARING IS ALL IT WILL TAKE FOR THOSE SIMPLE SOULS TO FORGET MY PAST TRANSGRESSIONS.
BUNIONS BEGONE
OH! WHAT'S THAT, DADDY?
APPARENTLY AN IRISH PODIATRIST, SON.
BUNIONS BEGONE
GLOUP
BUNIONS BEGONE
POC
THEN AGAIN, IF YOU'VE GOT THE LOOKS TO CARRY IT OFF, ENGLISH SQUIRE IS THE WAY TO GO!
SIBYL-ANNE
5 B

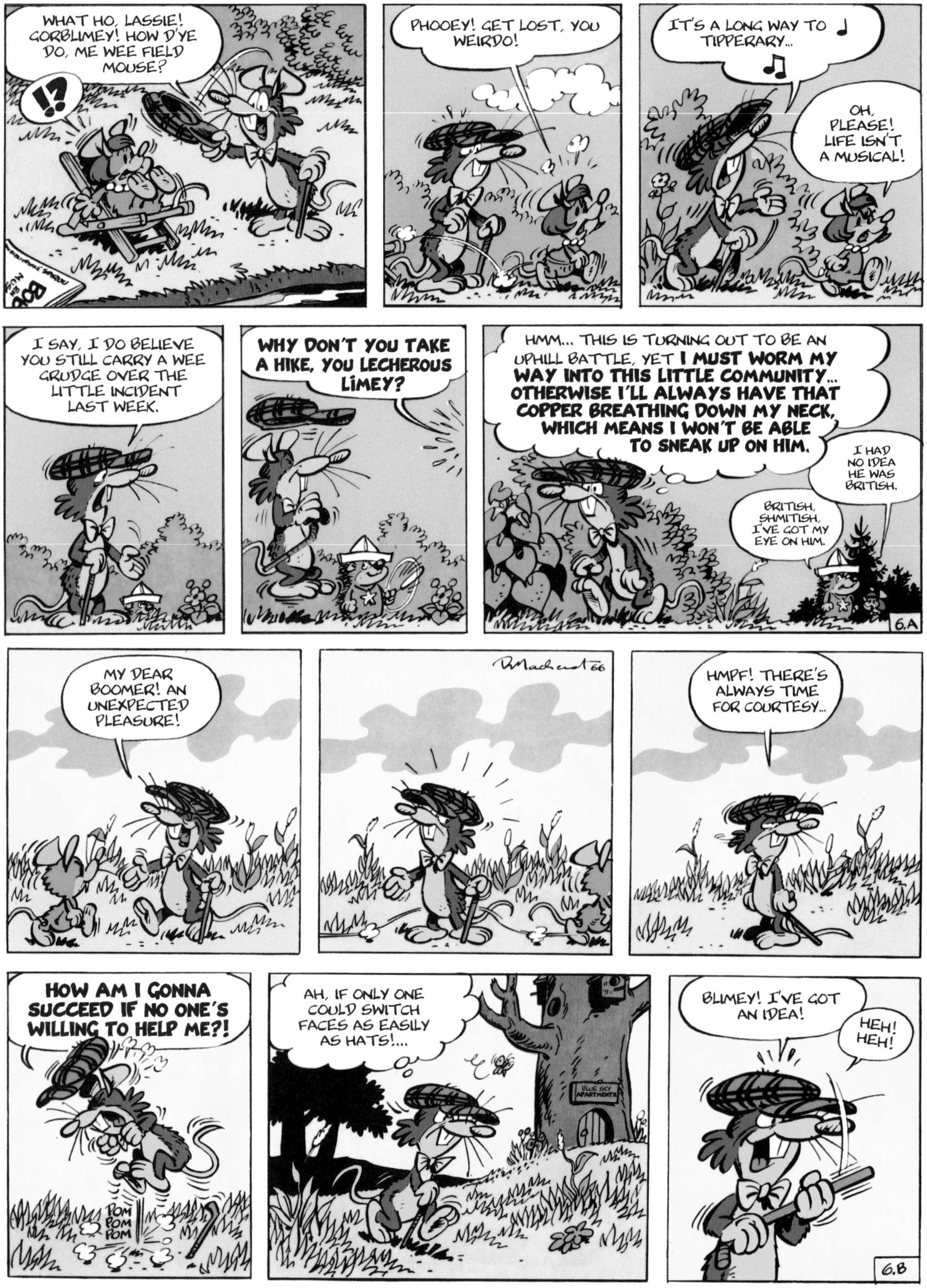
WHAT HO, LASSIE! GORBLIMEY! HOW D'YE DO, ME WEE FIELD MOUSE?
!?
PHOOEY! GET LOST, YOU WEIRDO!
IT'S A LONG WAY TO TIPPERARY...
OH, PLEASE! LIFE ISN'T A MUSICAL!
I SAY, I DO BELIEVE YOU STILL CARRY A WEE GRUDGE OVER THE LITTLE INCIDENT LAST WEEK.
WHY DON'T YOU TAKE A HIKE, YOU LECHEROUS LIMEY?
HMM... THIS IS TURNING OUT TO BE AN UPHILL BATTLE, YET I MUST WORM MY WAY INTO THIS LITTLE COMMUNITY... OTHERWISE I'LL ALWAYS HAVE THAT COPPER BREATHING DOWN MY NECK, WHICH MEANS I WON'T BE ABLE TO SNEAK UP ON HIM.
I HAD NO IDEA HE WAS BRITISH.
BRITISH, SHMITISH, I'VE GOT MY EYE ON HIM.
6.A
MY DEAR BOOMER! AN UNEXPECTED PLEASURE!
R Macherot 66
HMPF! THERE'S ALWAYS TIME FOR COURTESY...
HOW AM I GONNA SUCCEED IF NO ONE'S WILLING TO HELP ME?!
POM POM POM
AH, IF ONLY ONE COULD SWITCH FACES AS EASILY AS HATS!...
BLUE SKY APARTMENTS
BLIMEY! I'VE GOT AN IDEA!
HEH! HEH!
6.B

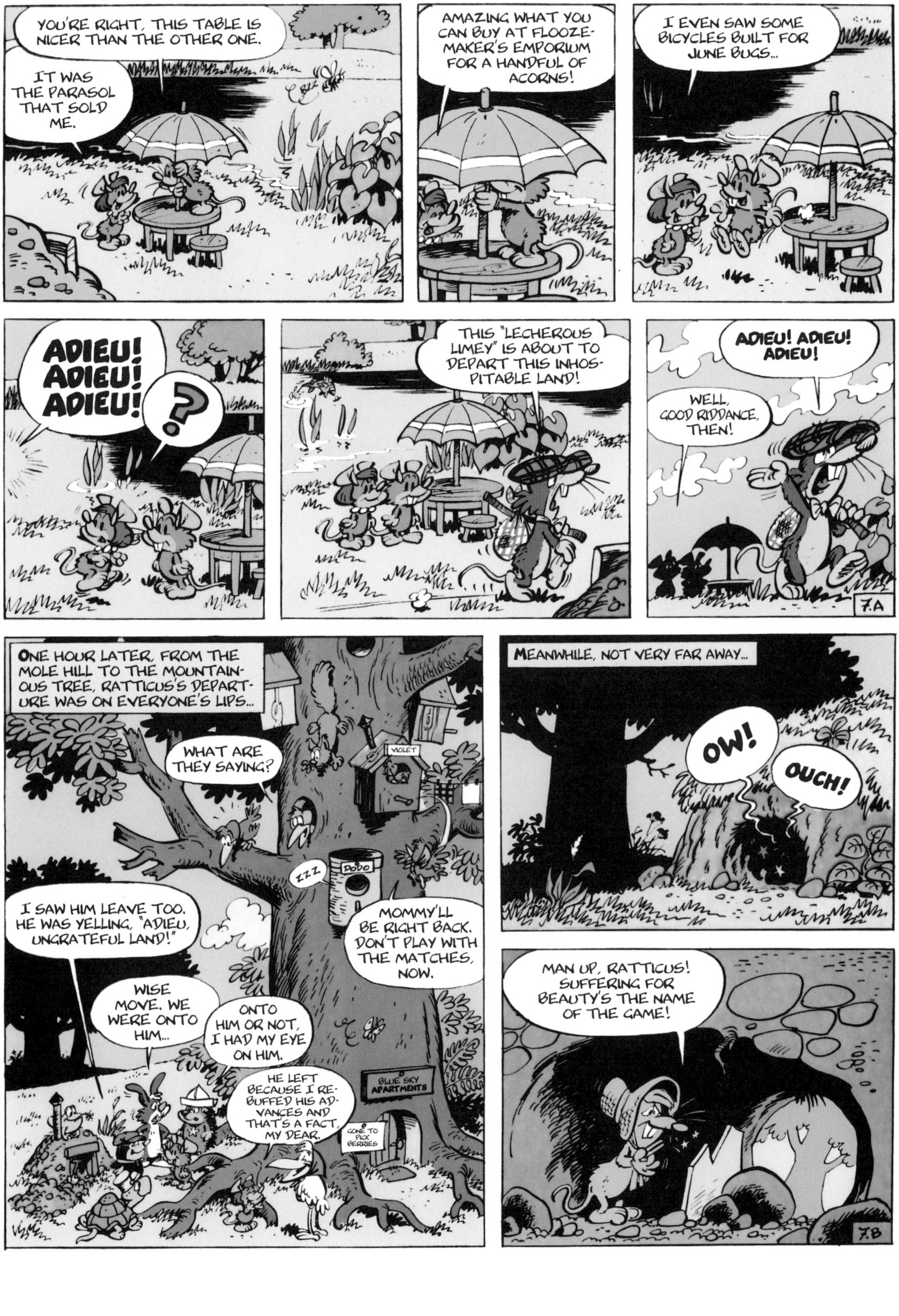

YOU'RE RIGHT, THIS TABLE IS NICER THAN THE OTHER ONE.
IT WAS THE PARASOL THAT SOLD ME.
AMAZING WHAT YOU CAN BUY AT FLOOZE-MAKER'S EMPORIUM FOR A HANDFUL OF ACORNS!
I EVEN SAW SOME BICYCLES BUILT FOR JUNE BUGS...
ADIEU! ADIEU! ADIEU!
?
THIS "LECHEROUS LIMEY" IS ABOUT TO DEPART THIS INHOS-PITABLE LAND!
ADIEU! ADIEU! ADIEU!
WELL, GOOD RIDDANCE, THEN!
7.A
ONE HOUR LATER, FROM THE MOLE HILL TO THE MOUNTAIN-OUS TREE, RATTICUS'S DEPART-URE WAS ON EVERYONE'S LIPS...
WHAT ARE THEY SAYING?
VIOLET
DODO
ZZZ
I SAW HIM LEAVE TOO. HE WAS YELLING, "ADIEU, UNGRATEFUL LAND!"
MOMMY'LL BE RIGHT BACK. DON'T PLAY WITH THE MATCHES, NOW.
WISE MOVE. WE WERE ONTO HIM...
ONTO HIM OR NOT, I HAD MY EYE ON HIM.
HE LEFT BECAUSE I RE-BUFFED HIS AD-VANCES AND THAT'S A FACT, MY DEAR.
BLUE SKY APARTMENTS
GONE TO PICK BERRIES
MEANWHILE, NOT VERY FAR AWAY...
OW!
OUCH!
MAN UP, RATTICUS! SUFFERING FOR BEAUTY'S THE NAME OF THE GAME!
7.B

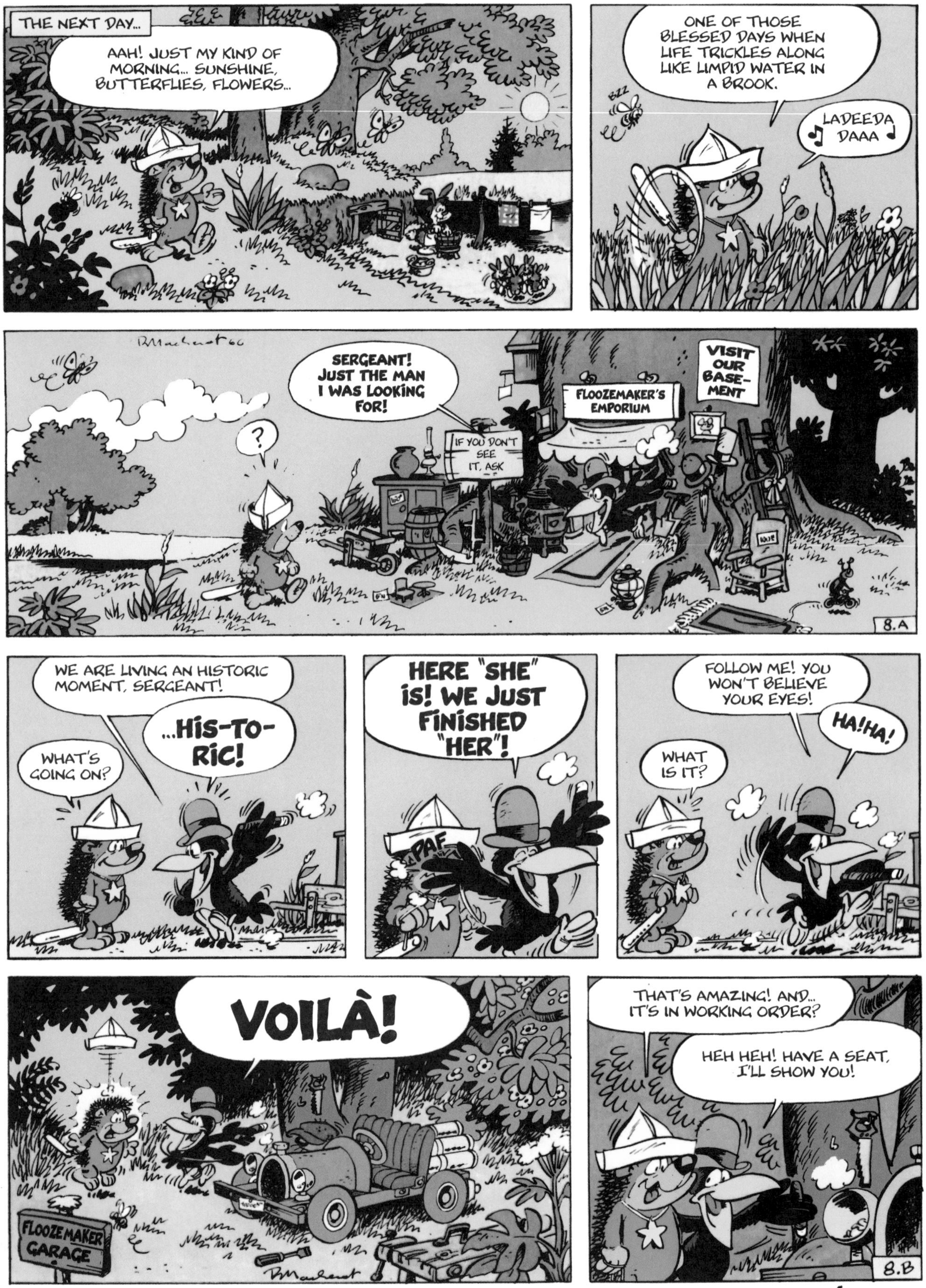
THE NEXT DAY...
AAH! JUST MY KIND OF MORNING... SUNSHINE, BUTTERFLIES, FLOWERS...
ONE OF THOSE BLESSED DAYS WHEN LIFE TRICKLES ALONG LIKE LIMPID WATER IN A BROOK.
BZZ
LADEEDA DAAA
SERGEANT! JUST THE MAN I WAS LOOKING FOR!
?
FLOOZEMAKER'S EMPORIUM
VISIT OUR BASEMENT
IF YOU DON'T SEE IT, ASK
8.A
WE ARE LIVING AN HISTORIC MOMENT, SERGEANT!
WHAT'S GOING ON?
...HIS-TO-RIC!
HERE "SHE" IS! WE JUST FINISHED "HER"!
PAF
FOLLOW ME! YOU WON'T BELIEVE YOUR EYES!
WHAT IS IT?
HA!HA!
VOILÀ!
FLOOZEMAKER GARAGE
THAT'S AMAZING! AND... IT'S IN WORKING ORDER?
HEH HEH! HAVE A SEAT, I'LL SHOW YOU!
8.B

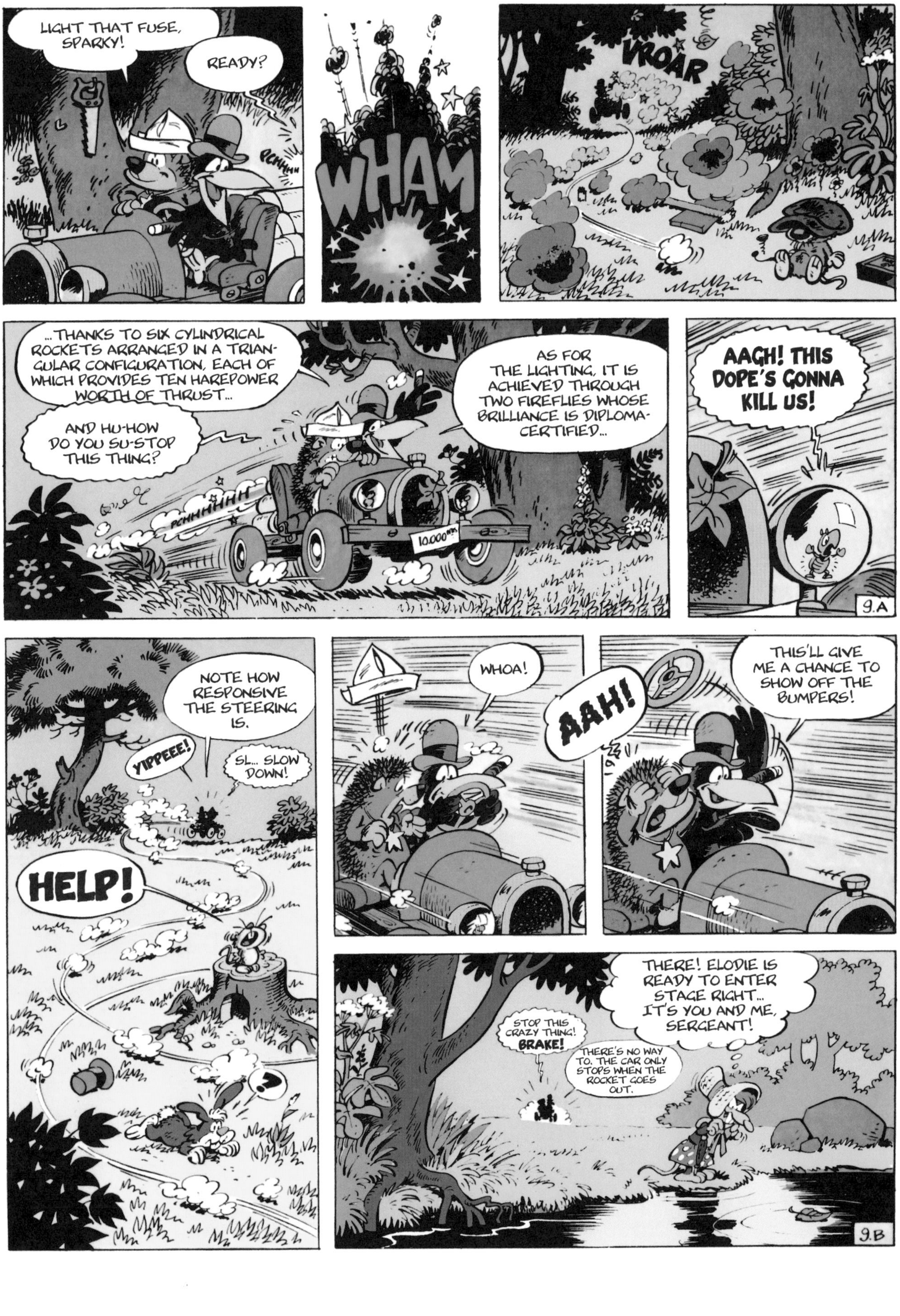
LIGHT THAT FUSE, SPARKY!
READY?
PCHHHHH
WHAM
VROAR
...THANKS TO SIX CYLINDRICAL ROCKETS ARRANGED IN A TRIANGULAR CONFIGURATION, EACH OF WHICH PROVIDES TEN HAREPOWER WORTH OF THRUST...
AND HU-HOW DO YOU SU-STOP THIS THING?
AS FOR THE LIGHTING, IT IS ACHIEVED THROUGH TWO FIREFLIES WHOSE BRILLIANCE IS DIPLOMA-CERTIFIED...
PCHHHHHH
10,000
AAGH! THIS DOPE'S GONNA KILL US!
9.A
NOTE HOW RESPONSIVE THE STEERING IS.
YIPPEEE!
SL... SLOW DOWN!
HELP!
?
WHOA!
AAH!
THIS'LL GIVE ME A CHANCE TO SHOW OFF THE BUMPERS!
THERE! ELODIE IS READY TO ENTER STAGE RIGHT... IT'S YOU AND ME, SERGEANT!
STOP THIS CRAZY THING! BRAKE!
THERE'S NO WAY TO. THE CAR ONLY STOPS WHEN THE ROCKET GOES OUT.
9.B

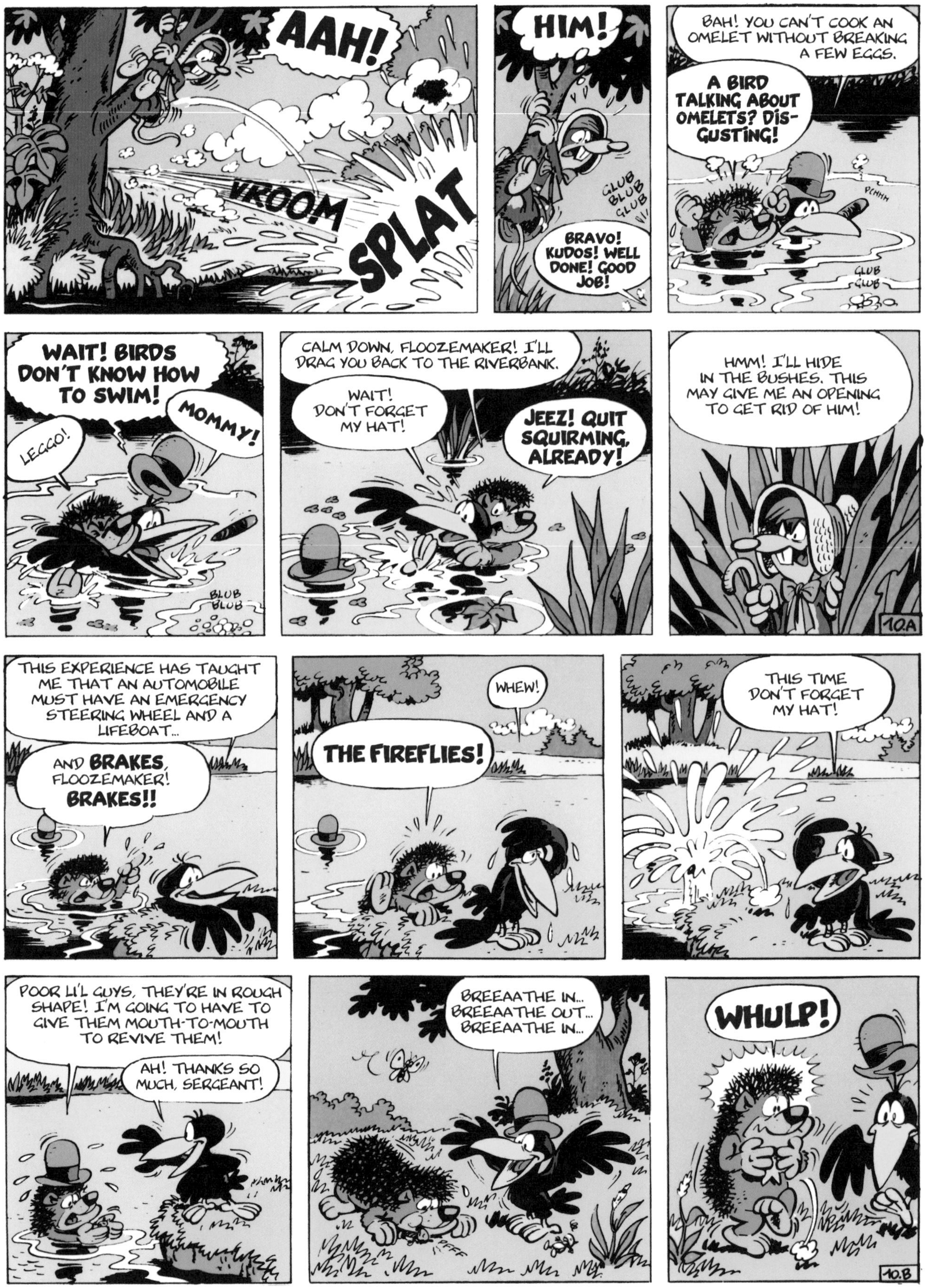
AAH!
VROOM
SPLAT
HIM!
GLUB BLUB GLUB
BRAVO! KUDOS! WELL DONE! GOOD JOB!
BAH! YOU CAN'T COOK AN OMELET WITHOUT BREAKING A FEW EGGS.
A BIRD TALKING ABOUT OMELETS? DISGUSTING!
GLUB GLUB
WAIT! BIRDS DON'T KNOW HOW TO SWIM!
LEGGO!
MOMMY!
BLUB BLUB
CALM DOWN, FLOOZEMAKER! I'LL DRAG YOU BACK TO THE RIVERBANK.
WAIT! DON'T FORGET MY HAT!
JEEZ! QUIT SQUIRMING, ALREADY!
HMM! I'LL HIDE IN THE BUSHES. THIS MAY GIVE ME AN OPENING TO GET RID OF HIM!
10.A
THIS EXPERIENCE HAS TAUGHT ME THAT AN AUTOMOBILE MUST HAVE AN EMERGENCY STEERING WHEEL AND A LIFEBOAT...
AND BRAKES, FLOOZEMAKER! BRAKES!!
WHEW!
THE FIREFLIES!
THIS TIME DON'T FORGET MY HAT!
POOR LI'L GUYS, THEY'RE IN ROUGH SHAPE! I'M GOING TO HAVE TO GIVE THEM MOUTH-TO-MOUTH TO REVIVE THEM!
AH! THANKS SO MUCH, SERGEANT!
BREEAATHE IN... BREEAATHE OUT... BREEAATHE IN...
WHULP!
10.B

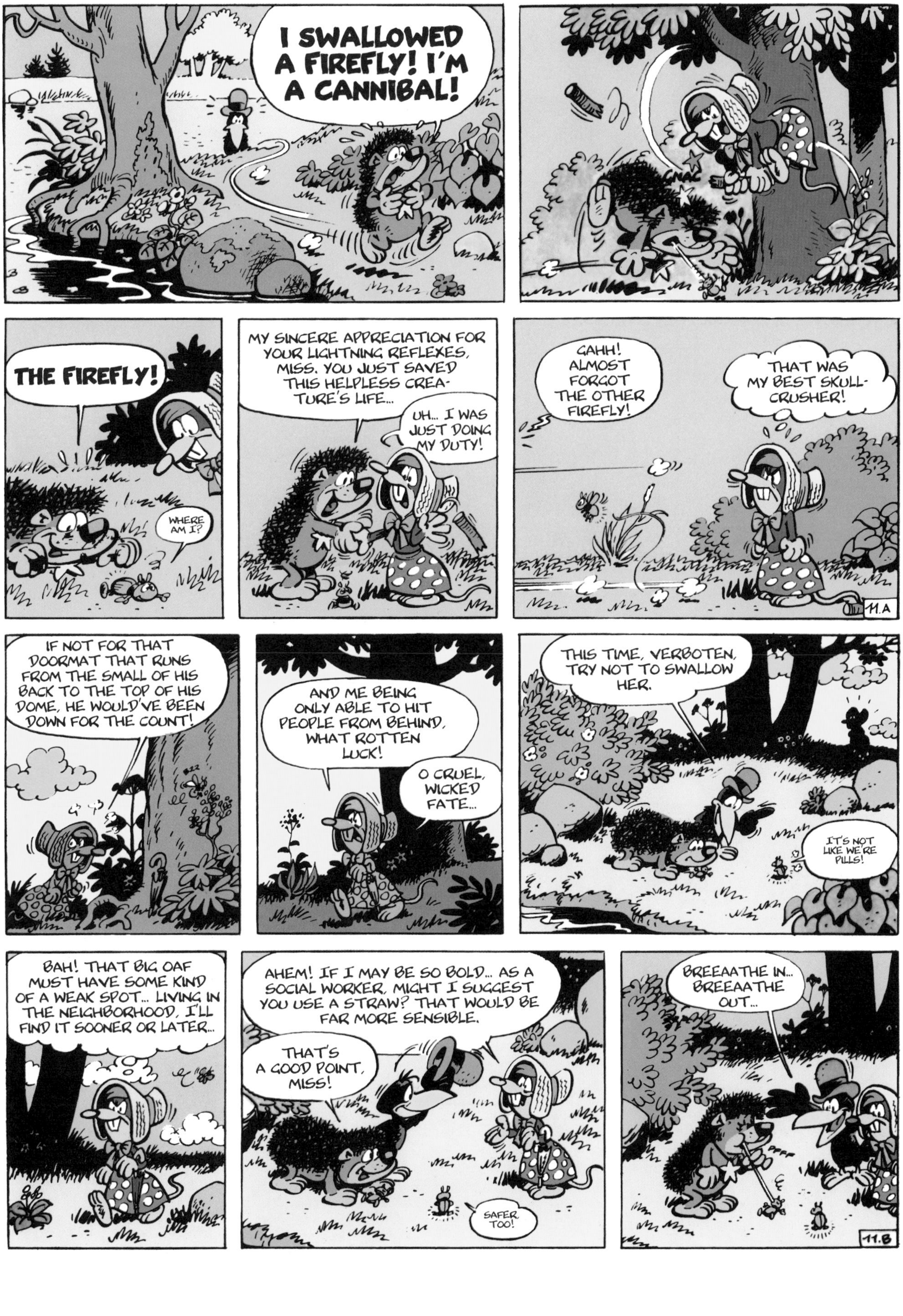
I SWALLOWED A FIREFLY! I'M A CANNIBAL!
THE FIREFLY!
WHERE AM I?
MY SINCERE APPRECIATION FOR YOUR LIGHTNING REFLEXES, MISS. YOU JUST SAVED THIS HELPLESS CREATURE'S LIFE...
UH... I WAS JUST DOING MY DUTY!
GAHH! ALMOST FORGOT THE OTHER FIREFLY!
THAT WAS MY BEST SKULL-CRUSHER!
11.A
IF NOT FOR THAT DOORMAT THAT RUNS FROM THE SMALL OF HIS BACK TO THE TOP OF HIS DOME, HE WOULD'VE BEEN DOWN FOR THE COUNT!
AND ME BEING ONLY ABLE TO HIT PEOPLE FROM BEHIND, WHAT ROTTEN LUCK!
O CRUEL, WICKED FATE...
THIS TIME, VERBOTEN, TRY NOT TO SWALLOW HER.
IT'S NOT LIKE WE'RE PILLS!
BAH! THAT BIG OAF MUST HAVE SOME KIND OF A WEAK SPOT... LIVING IN THE NEIGHBORHOOD, I'LL FIND IT SOONER OR LATER...
AHEM! IF I MAY BE SO BOLD... AS A SOCIAL WORKER, MIGHT I SUGGEST YOU USE A STRAW? THAT WOULD BE FAR MORE SENSIBLE.
THAT'S A GOOD POINT, MISS!
SAFER, TOO!
BREEAATHE IN... BREEAATHE OUT...
11.B

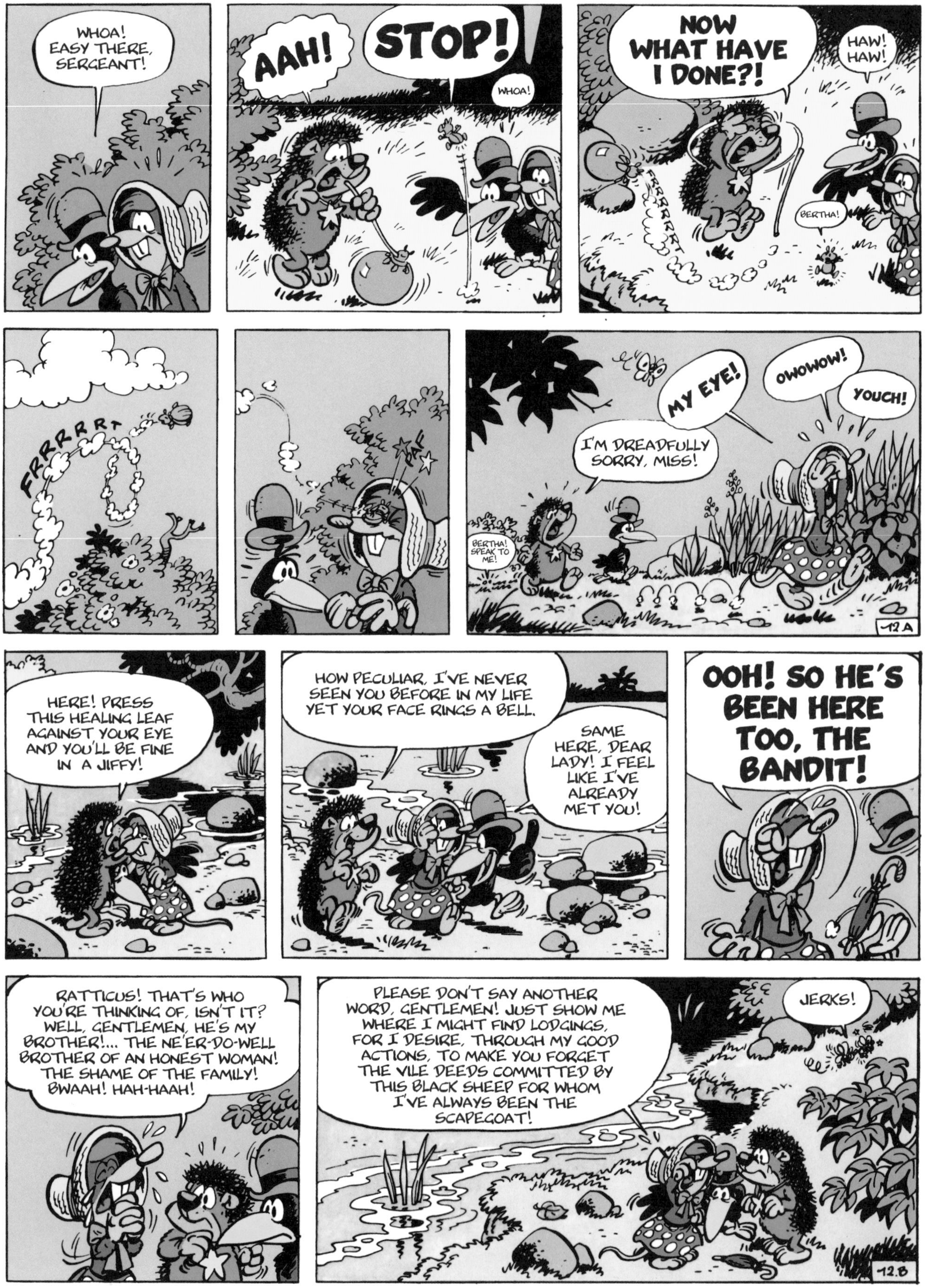
WHOA! EASY THERE, SERGEANT!
AAH!
STOP!
WHOA!
NOW WHAT HAVE I DONE?!
HAW! HAW!
FRRRRRT
BERTHA!
FRRRRRT
I'M DREADFULLY SORRY, MISS!
MY EYE!
OWOWOW!
YOUCH!
BERTHA! SPEAK TO ME!
12 A
HERE! PRESS THIS HEALING LEAF AGAINST YOUR EYE AND YOU'LL BE FINE IN A JIFFY!
HOW PECULIAR, I'VE NEVER SEEN YOU BEFORE IN MY LIFE YET YOUR FACE RINGS A BELL.
SAME HERE, DEAR LADY! I FEEL LIKE I'VE ALREADY MET YOU!
OOH! SO HE'S BEEN HERE TOO, THE BANDIT!
RATTICUS! THAT'S WHO YOU'RE THINKING OF, ISN'T IT? WELL, GENTLEMEN, HE'S MY BROTHER!... THE NE'ER-DO-WELL BROTHER OF AN HONEST WOMAN! THE SHAME OF THE FAMILY! BWAAH! HAH-HAAH!
PLEASE DON'T SAY ANOTHER WORD, GENTLEMEN! JUST SHOW ME WHERE I MIGHT FIND LODGINGS, FOR I DESIRE, THROUGH MY GOOD ACTIONS, TO MAKE YOU FORGET THE VILE DEEDS COMMITTED BY THIS BLACK SHEEP FOR WHOM I'VE ALWAYS BEEN THE SCAPEGOAT!
JERKS!
12 B

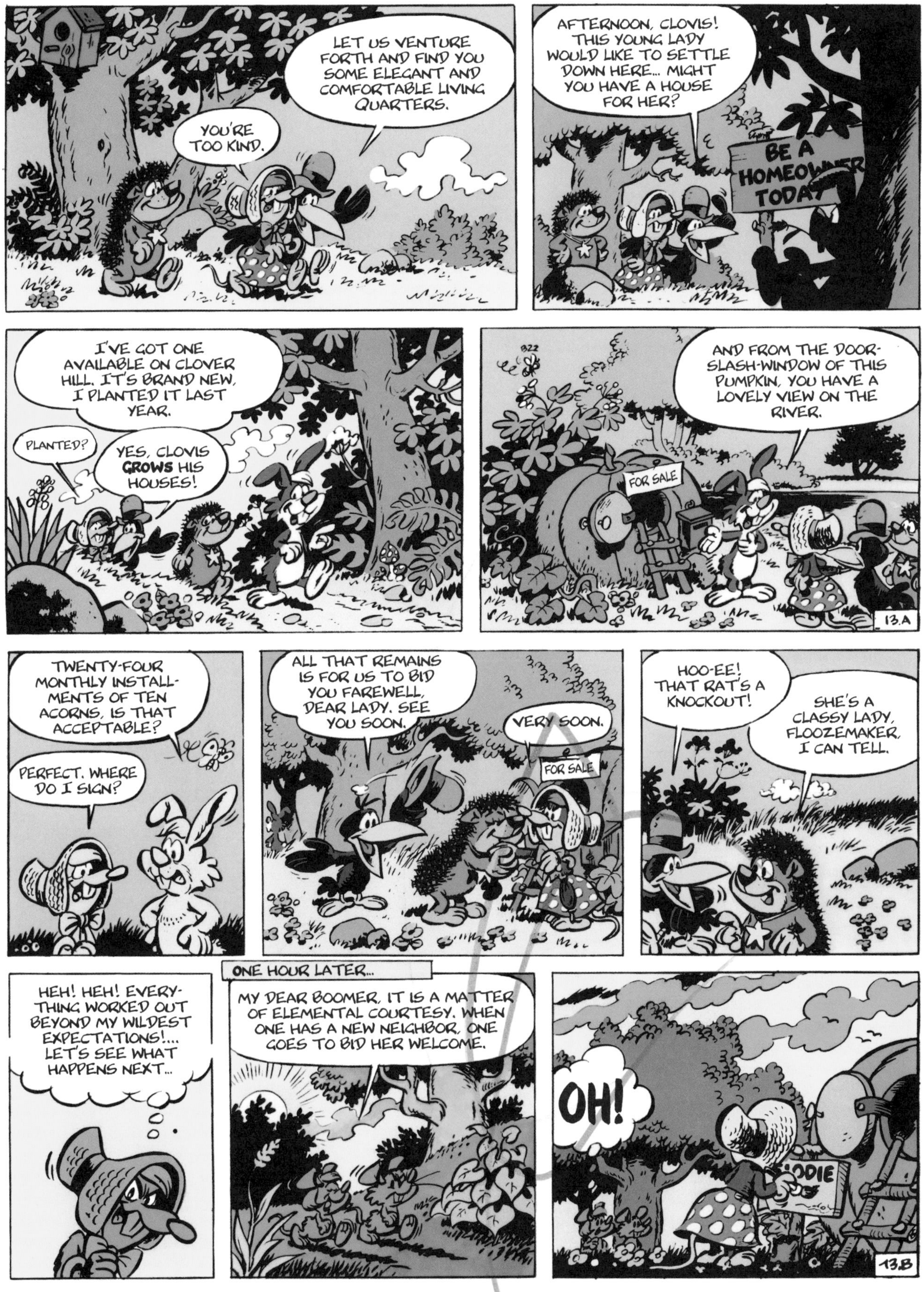
LET US VENTURE FORTH AND FIND YOU SOME ELEGANT AND COMFORTABLE LIVING QUARTERS.
YOU'RE TOO KIND.
AFTERNOON, CLOVIS! THIS YOUNG LADY WOULD LIKE TO SETTLE DOWN HERE... MIGHT YOU HAVE A HOUSE FOR HER?
BE A HOMEOWNER TODAY
I'VE GOT ONE AVAILABLE ON CLOVER HILL. IT'S BRAND NEW, I PLANTED IT LAST YEAR.
PLANTED?
YES, CLOVIS **GROWS** HIS HOUSES!
BZZ
AND FROM THE DOOR-SLASH-WINDOW OF THIS PUMPKIN, YOU HAVE A LOVELY VIEW ON THE RIVER.
FOR SALE
13.A
TWENTY-FOUR MONTHLY INSTALL-MENTS OF TEN ACORNS, IS THAT ACCEPTABLE?
PERFECT. WHERE DO I SIGN?
ALL THAT REMAINS IS FOR US TO BID YOU FAREWELL, DEAR LADY. SEE YOU SOON.
VERY SOON.
FOR SALE
HOO-EE! THAT RAT'S A KNOCKOUT!
SHE'S A CLASSY LADY, FLOOZEMAKER. I CAN TELL.
HEH! HEH! EVERY-THING WORKED OUT BEYOND MY WILDEST EXPECTATIONS!... LET'S SEE WHAT HAPPENS NEXT...
ONE HOUR LATER...
MY DEAR BOOMER, IT IS A MATTER OF ELEMENTAL COURTESY. WHEN ONE HAS A NEW NEIGHBOR, ONE GOES TO BID HER WELCOME.
OH!
13.B

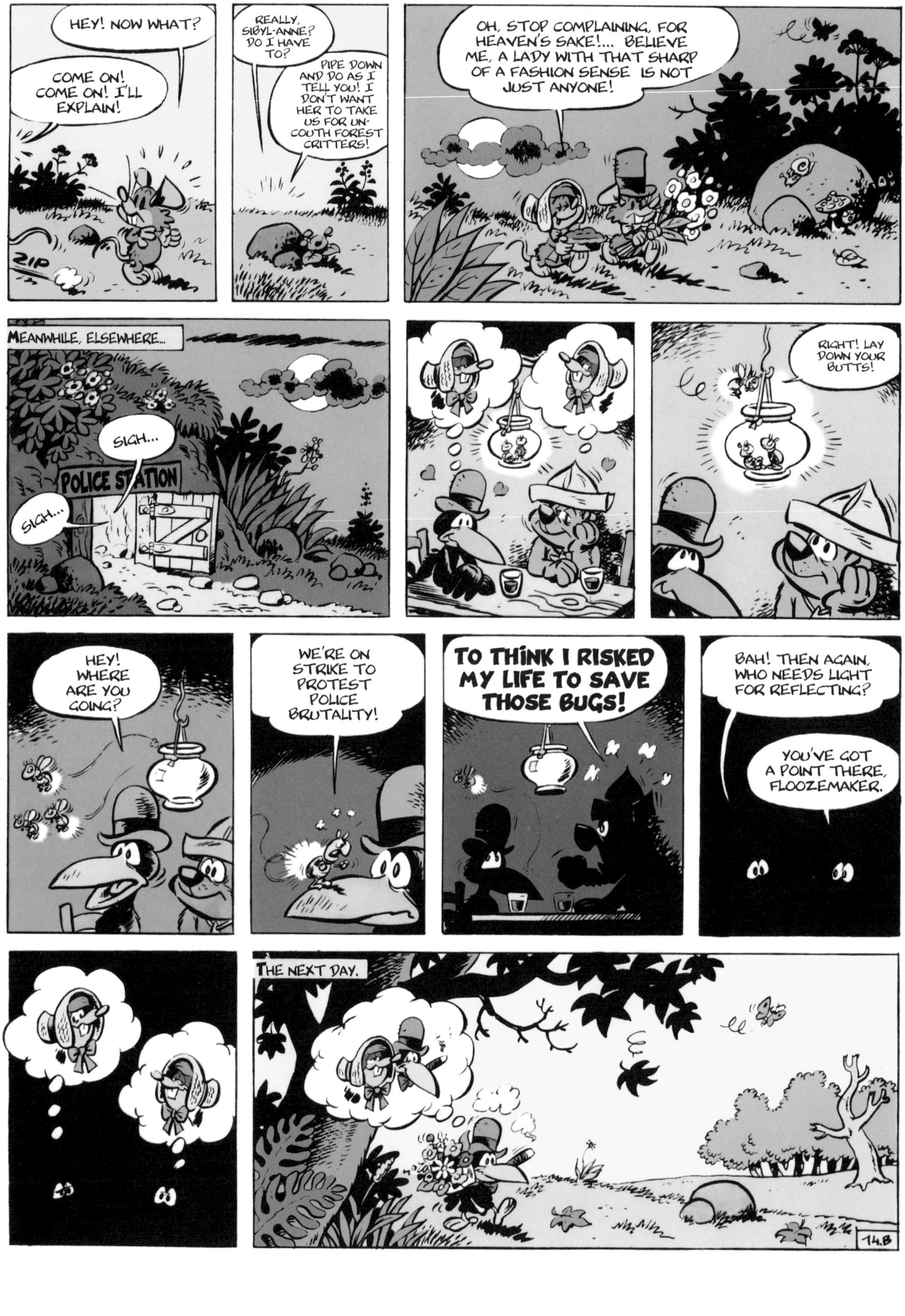

HEY! NOW WHAT?
COME ON! COME ON! I'LL EXPLAIN!
ZIP
REALLY, SIBYL-ANNE? DO I HAVE TO?
PIPE DOWN AND DO AS I TELL YOU! I DON'T WANT HER TO TAKE US FOR UNCOUTH FOREST CRITTERS!
OH, STOP COMPLAINING, FOR HEAVEN'S SAKE!.... BELIEVE ME, A LADY WITH THAT SHARP OF A FASHION SENSE IS NOT JUST ANYONE!
MEANWHILE, ELSEWHERE...
SIGH...
POLICE STATION
SIGH...
RIGHT! LAY DOWN YOUR BUTTS!
HEY! WHERE ARE YOU GOING?
WE'RE ON STRIKE TO PROTEST POLICE BRUTALITY!
TO THINK I RISKED MY LIFE TO SAVE THOSE BUGS!
BAH! THEN AGAIN, WHO NEEDS LIGHT FOR REFLECTING?
YOU'VE GOT A POINT THERE, FLOOZEMAKER.
THE NEXT DAY.
14.B

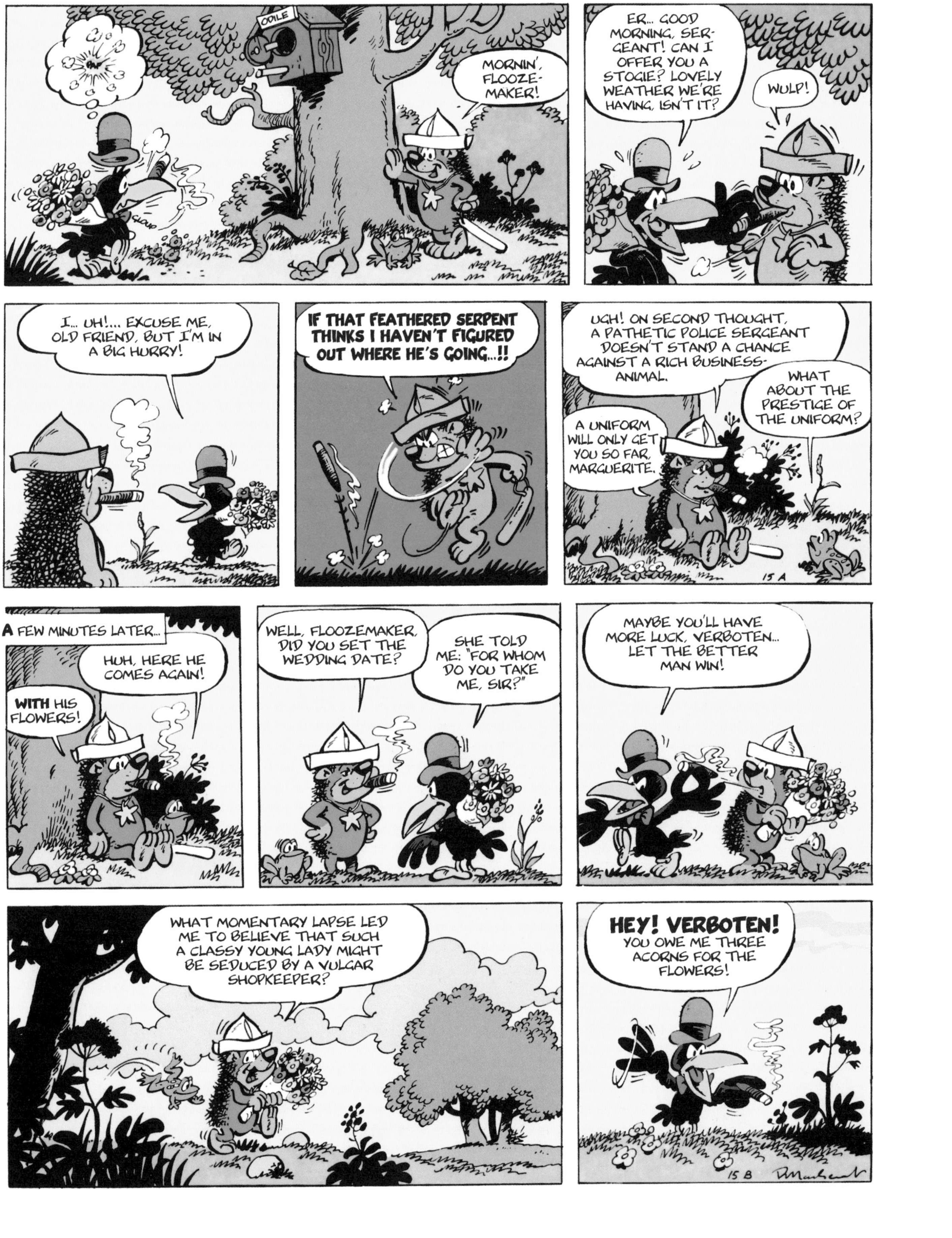
ODILE
MORNIN', FLOOZE-MAKER!
ER... GOOD MORNING, SER-GEANT! CAN I OFFER YOU A STOGIE? LOVELY WEATHER WE'RE HAVING, ISN'T IT?
WULP!
I... UH!... EXCUSE ME, OLD FRIEND, BUT I'M IN A BIG HURRY!
IF THAT FEATHERED SERPENT THINKS I HAVEN'T FIGURED OUT WHERE HE'S GOING...!!
UGH! ON SECOND THOUGHT, A PATHETIC POLICE SERGEANT DOESN'T STAND A CHANCE AGAINST A RICH BUSINESS-ANIMAL.
WHAT ABOUT THE PRESTIGE OF THE UNIFORM?
A UNIFORM WILL ONLY GET YOU SO FAR, MARGUERITE.
15 A
A FEW MINUTES LATER...
HUH, HERE HE COMES AGAIN!
WITH HIS FLOWERS!
WELL, FLOOZEMAKER, DID YOU SET THE WEDDING DATE?
SHE TOLD ME: "FOR WHOM DO YOU TAKE ME, SIR?"
MAYBE YOU'LL HAVE MORE LUCK, VERBOTEN... LET THE BETTER MAN WIN!
WHAT MOMENTARY LAPSE LED ME TO BELIEVE THAT SUCH A CLASSY YOUNG LADY MIGHT BE SEDUCED BY A VULGAR SHOPKEEPER?
HEY! VERBOTEN! YOU OWE ME THREE ACORNS FOR THE FLOWERS!
15 B

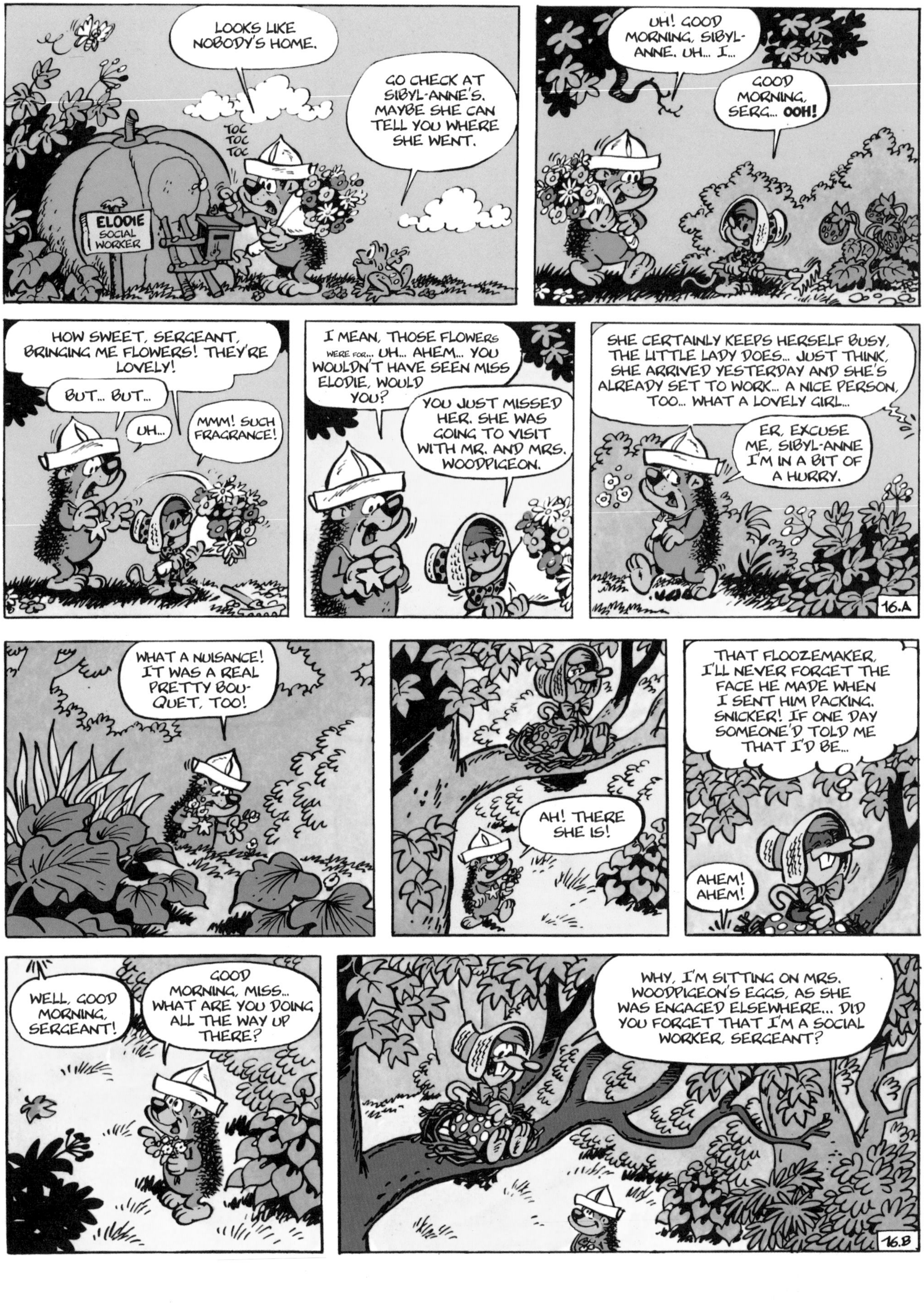
LOOKS LIKE NOBODY'S HOME.
TOC TOC TOC
ELODIE SOCIAL WORKER
GO CHECK AT SIBYL-ANNE'S. MAYBE SHE CAN TELL YOU WHERE SHE WENT.
UH! GOOD MORNING, SIBYL-ANNE. UH... I...
GOOD MORNING, SERG... OOH!
HOW SWEET, SERGEANT, BRINGING ME FLOWERS! THEY'RE LOVELY!
BUT... BUT...
UH...
MMM! SUCH FRAGRANCE!
I MEAN, THOSE FLOWERS WERE FOR... UH... AHEM... YOU WOULDN'T HAVE SEEN MISS ELODIE, WOULD YOU?
YOU JUST MISSED HER. SHE WAS GOING TO VISIT WITH MR. AND MRS. WOODPIGEON.
SHE CERTAINLY KEEPS HERSELF BUSY, THE LITTLE LADY DOES... JUST THINK, SHE ARRIVED YESTERDAY AND SHE'S ALREADY SET TO WORK... A NICE PERSON, TOO... WHAT A LOVELY GIRL...
ER, EXCUSE ME, SIBYL-ANNE I'M IN A BIT OF A HURRY.
16.A
WHAT A NUISANCE! IT WAS A REAL PRETTY BOU-QUET, TOO!
AH! THERE SHE IS!
THAT FLOOZEMAKER, I'LL NEVER FORGET THE FACE HE MADE WHEN I SENT HIM PACKING. SNICKER! IF ONE DAY SOMEONE'D TOLD ME THAT I'D BE...
AHEM! AHEM!
WELL, GOOD MORNING, SERGEANT!
GOOD MORNING, MISS... WHAT ARE YOU DOING ALL THE WAY UP THERE?
WHY, I'M SITTING ON MRS. WOODPIGEON'S EGGS, AS SHE WAS ENGAGED ELSEWHERE... DID YOU FORGET THAT I'M A SOCIAL WORKER, SERGEANT?
16.B

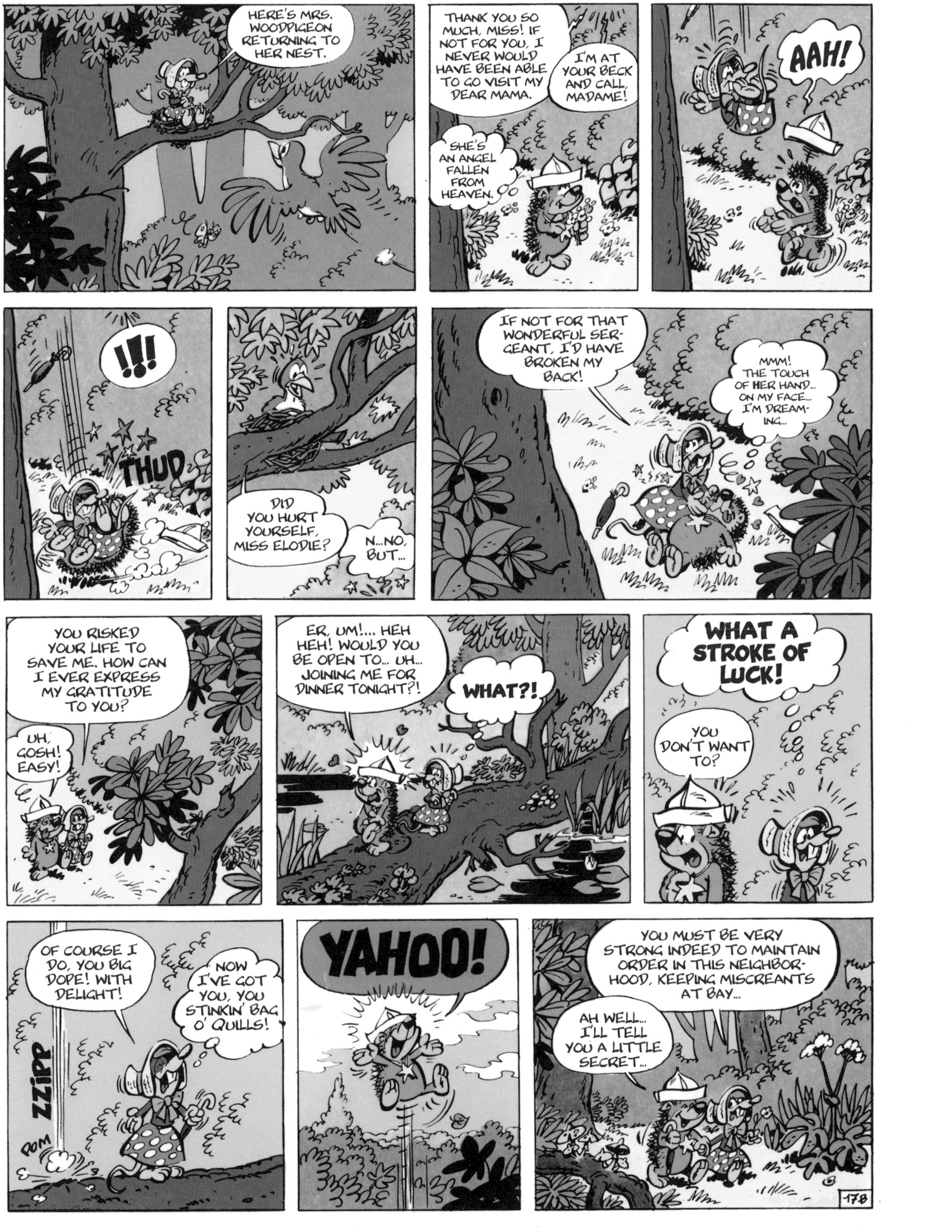
HERE'S MRS. WOODPIGEON RETURNING TO HER NEST.
THANK YOU SO MUCH, MISS! IF NOT FOR YOU, I NEVER WOULD HAVE BEEN ABLE TO GO VISIT MY DEAR MAMA.
I'M AT YOUR BECK AND CALL, MADAME!
SHE'S AN ANGEL FALLEN FROM HEAVEN.
AAH!
!!!
THUD
DID YOU HURT YOURSELF, MISS ELODIE?
N...NO, BUT...
IF NOT FOR THAT WONDERFUL SERGEANT, I'D HAVE BROKEN MY BACK!
MMM! THE TOUCH OF HER HAND... ON MY FACE... I'M DREAMING...
YOU RISKED YOUR LIFE TO SAVE ME. HOW CAN I EVER EXPRESS MY GRATITUDE TO YOU?
UH, GOSH! EASY!
ER, UM!... HEH HEH! WOULD YOU BE OPEN TO... UH... JOINING ME FOR DINNER TONIGHT?!
WHAT?!
WHAT A STROKE OF LUCK!
YOU DON'T WANT TO?
OF COURSE I DO, YOU BIG DOPE! WITH DELIGHT!
NOW I'VE GOT YOU, YOU STINKIN' BAG O' QUILLS!
ZZIPP
POM
YAHOO!
YOU MUST BE VERY STRONG INDEED TO MAINTAIN ORDER IN THIS NEIGHBORHOOD, KEEPING MISCREANTS AT BAY...
AH WELL... I'LL TELL YOU A LITTLE SECRET...
17-B

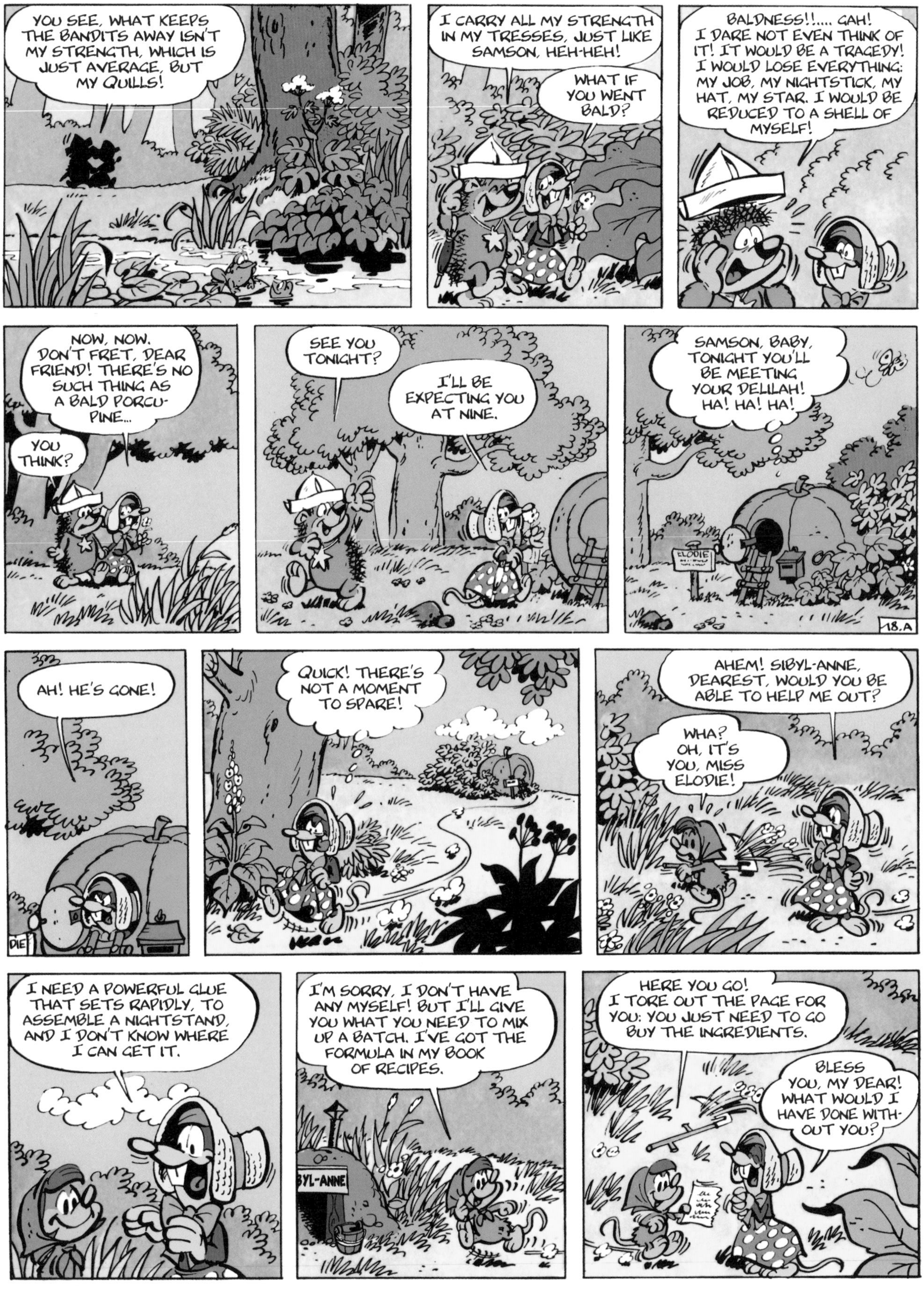
YOU SEE, WHAT KEEPS THE BANDITS AWAY ISN'T MY STRENGTH, WHICH IS JUST AVERAGE, BUT MY QUILLS!
I CARRY ALL MY STRENGTH IN MY TRESSES, JUST LIKE SAMSON, HEH-HEH!
WHAT IF YOU WENT BALD?
BALDNESS!!.... GAH! I DARE NOT EVEN THINK OF IT! IT WOULD BE A TRAGEDY! I WOULD LOSE EVERYTHING: MY JOB, MY NIGHTSTICK, MY HAT, MY STAR. I WOULD BE REDUCED TO A SHELL OF MYSELF!
NOW, NOW. DON'T FRET, DEAR FRIEND! THERE'S NO SUCH THING AS A BALD PORCUPINE...
YOU THINK?
SEE YOU TONIGHT?
I'LL BE EXPECTING YOU AT NINE.
SAMSON, BABY, TONIGHT YOU'LL BE MEETING YOUR DELILAH! HA! HA! HA!
ELODIE
18.A
AH! HE'S GONE!
DIE
QUICK! THERE'S NOT A MOMENT TO SPARE!
AHEM! SIBYL-ANNE, DEAREST, WOULD YOU BE ABLE TO HELP ME OUT?
WHA? OH, IT'S YOU, MISS ELODIE!
I NEED A POWERFUL GLUE THAT SETS RAPIDLY, TO ASSEMBLE A NIGHTSTAND, AND I DON'T KNOW WHERE I CAN GET IT.
I'M SORRY, I DON'T HAVE ANY MYSELF! BUT I'LL GIVE YOU WHAT YOU NEED TO MIX UP A BATCH. I'VE GOT THE FORMULA IN MY BOOK OF RECIPES.
BYL-ANNE
HERE YOU GO! I TORE OUT THE PAGE FOR YOU: YOU JUST NEED TO GO BUY THE INGREDIENTS.
BLESS YOU, MY DEAR! WHAT WOULD I HAVE DONE WITHOUT YOU?

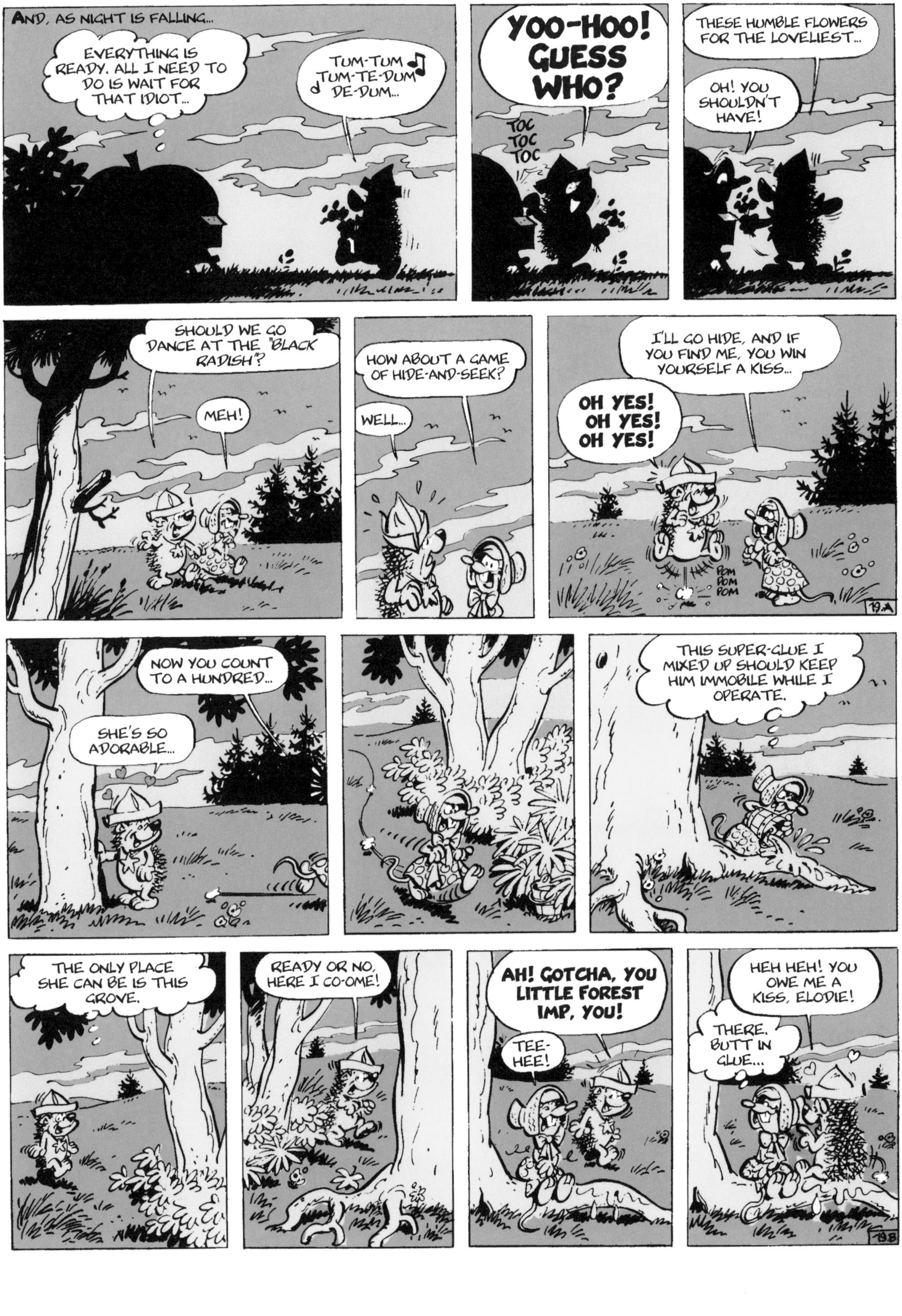
AND, AS NIGHT IS FALLING...
EVERYTHING IS READY. ALL I NEED TO DO IS WAIT FOR THAT IDIOT...
TUM-TUM TUM-TE-DUM DE-DUM...
YOO-HOO! GUESS WHO?
TOC TOC TOC
THESE HUMBLE FLOWERS FOR THE LOVELIEST...
OH! YOU SHOULDN'T HAVE!
SHOULD WE GO DANCE AT THE "BLACK RADISH"?
MEH!
HOW ABOUT A GAME OF HIDE-AND-SEEK?
WELL...
I'LL GO HIDE, AND IF YOU FIND ME, YOU WIN YOURSELF A KISS...
OH YES! OH YES! OH YES!
POM POM POM
NOW YOU COUNT TO A HUNDRED...
SHE'S SO ADORABLE...
THIS SUPER-GLUE I MIXED UP SHOULD KEEP HIM IMMOBILE WHILE I OPERATE.
THE ONLY PLACE SHE CAN BE IS THIS GROVE.
READY OR NO, HERE I CO-OME!
AH! GOTCHA, YOU LITTLE FOREST IMP, YOU!
TEE-HEE!
HEH HEH! YOU OWE ME A KISS, ELODIE!
THERE. BUTT IN GLUE...

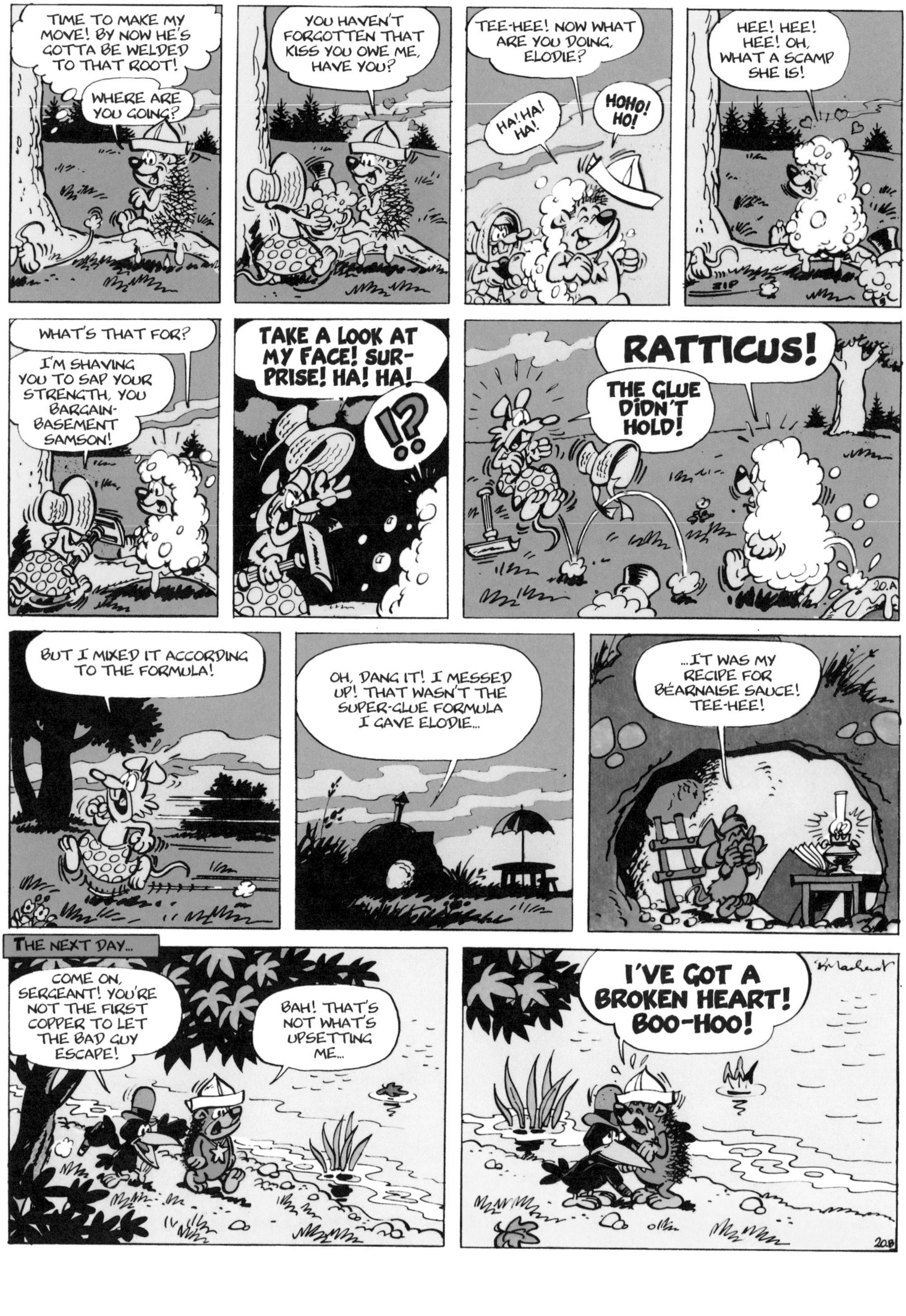

TIME TO MAKE MY MOVE! BY NOW HE'S GOTTA BE WELDED TO THAT ROOT!
WHERE ARE YOU GOING?
YOU HAVEN'T FORGOTTEN THAT KISS YOU OWE ME, HAVE YOU?
TEE-HEE! NOW WHAT ARE YOU DOING, ELODIE?
HA! HA! HA!
HOHO! HO!
HEE! HEE! HEE! OH, WHAT A SCAMP SHE IS!
ZIP
WHAT'S THAT FOR?
I'M SHAVING YOU TO SAP YOUR STRENGTH, YOU BARGAIN-BASEMENT SAMSON!
TAKE A LOOK AT MY FACE! SURPRISE! HA! HA!
!?
RATTICUS!
THE GLUE DIDN'T HOLD!
20.A
BUT I MIXED IT ACCORDING TO THE FORMULA!
OH, DANG IT! I MESSED UP! THAT WASN'T THE SUPER-GLUE FORMULA I GAVE ELODIE...
...IT WAS MY RECIPE FOR BÉARNAISE SAUCE! TEE-HEE!
THE NEXT DAY...
COME ON, SERGEANT! YOU'RE NOT THE FIRST COPPER TO LET THE BAD GUY ESCAPE!
BAH! THAT'S NOT WHAT'S UPSETTING ME...
I'VE GOT A BROKEN HEART! BOO-HOO!
20.B

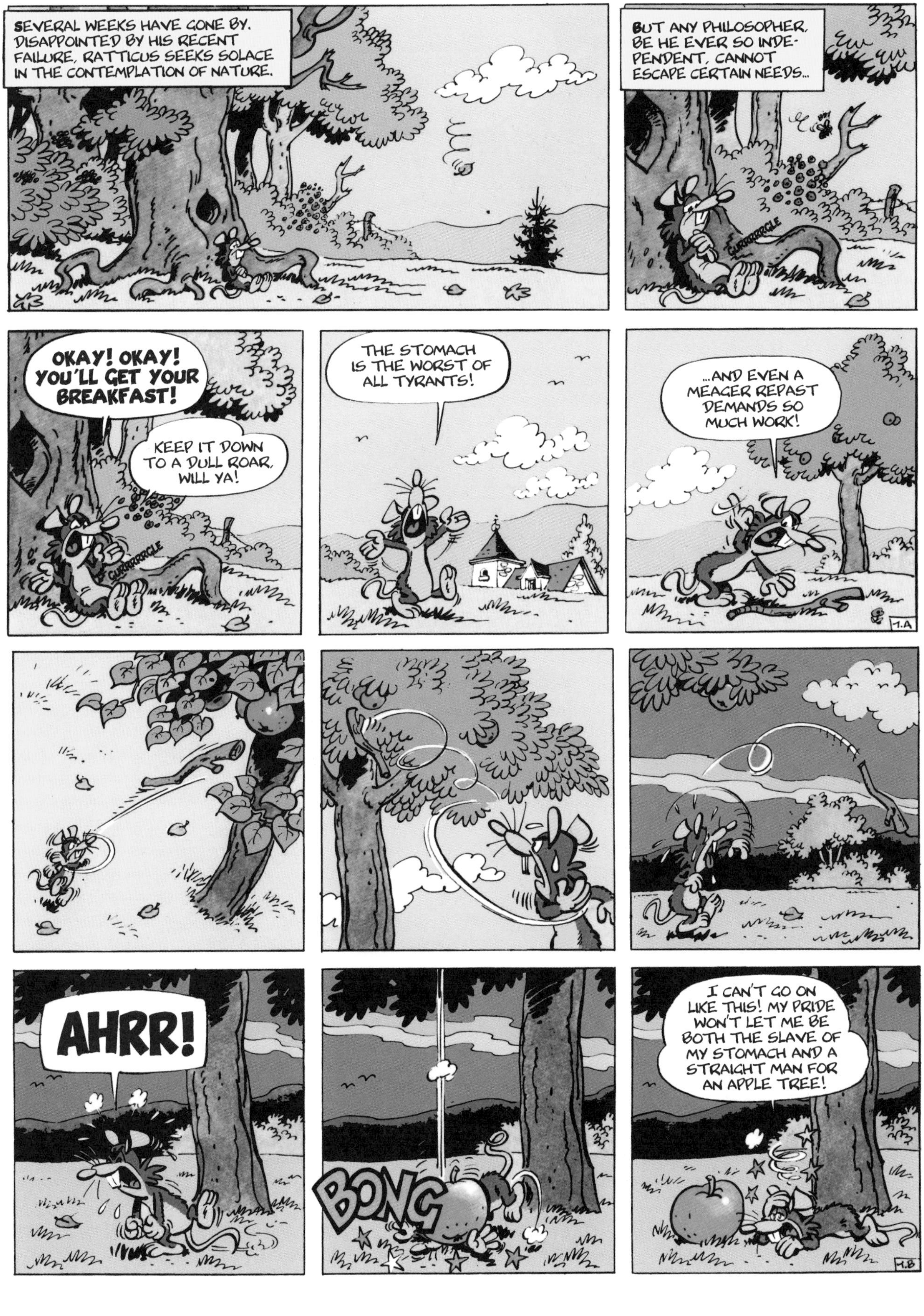
SEVERAL WEEKS HAVE GONE BY. DISAPPOINTED BY HIS RECENT FAILURE, RATTICUS SEEKS SOLACE IN THE CONTEMPLATION OF NATURE.
BUT ANY PHILOSOPHER, BE HE EVER SO INDEPENDENT, CANNOT ESCAPE CERTAIN NEEDS...
GURRRRRGLE
OKAY! OKAY! YOU'LL GET YOUR BREAKFAST!
KEEP IT DOWN TO A DULL ROAR, WILL YA!
GURRRRRGLE
THE STOMACH IS THE WORST OF ALL TYRANTS!
...AND EVEN A MEAGER REPAST DEMANDS SO MUCH WORK!
AHRR!
BONG
I CAN'T GO ON LIKE THIS! MY PRIDE WON'T LET ME BE BOTH THE SLAVE OF MY STOMACH AND A STRAIGHT MAN FOR AN APPLE TREE!

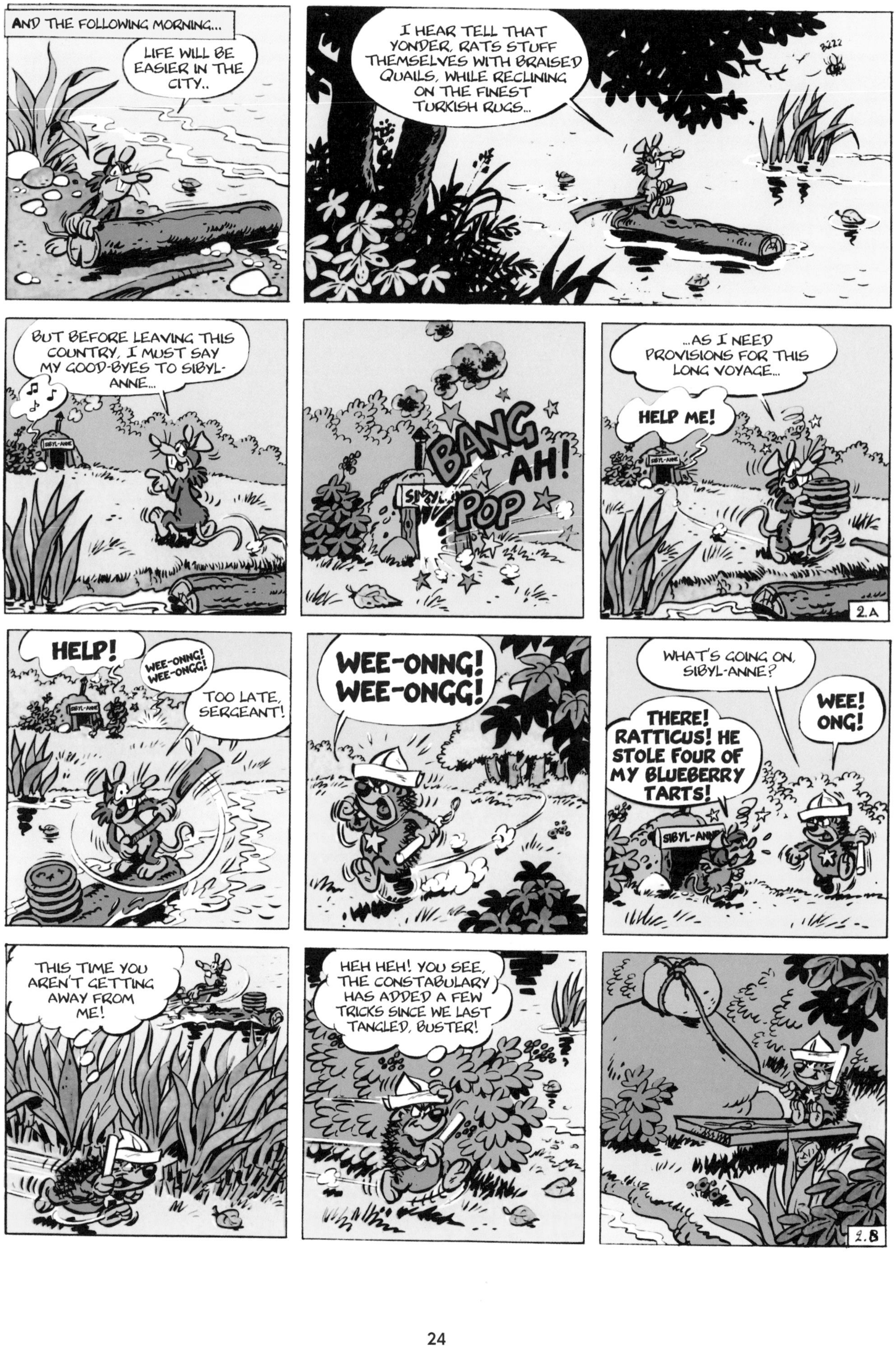
AND THE FOLLOWING MORNING...
LIFE WILL BE EASIER IN THE CITY..
I HEAR TELL THAT YONDER, RATS STUFF THEMSELVES WITH BRAISED QUAILS, WHILE RECLINING ON THE FINEST TURKISH RUGS...
BZZZ
BUT BEFORE LEAVING THIS COUNTRY, I MUST SAY MY GOOD-BYES TO SIBYL-ANNE...
SIBYL-ANNE
BANG
AH!
POP
...AS I NEED PROVISIONS FOR THIS LONG VOYAGE...
HELP ME!
SIBYL-ANNE
2.A
HELP!
WEE-ONNG! WEE-ONGG!
TOO LATE, SERGEANT!
SIBYL-ANNE
WEE-ONNG! WEE-ONGG!
WHAT'S GOING ON, SIBYL-ANNE?
THERE! RATTICUS! HE STOLE FOUR OF MY BLUEBERRY TARTS!
WEE! ONG!
SIBYL-ANNE
THIS TIME YOU AREN'T GETTING AWAY FROM ME!
HEH HEH! YOU SEE, THE CONSTABULARY HAS ADDED A FEW TRICKS SINCE WE LAST TANGLED, BUSTER!
2.B

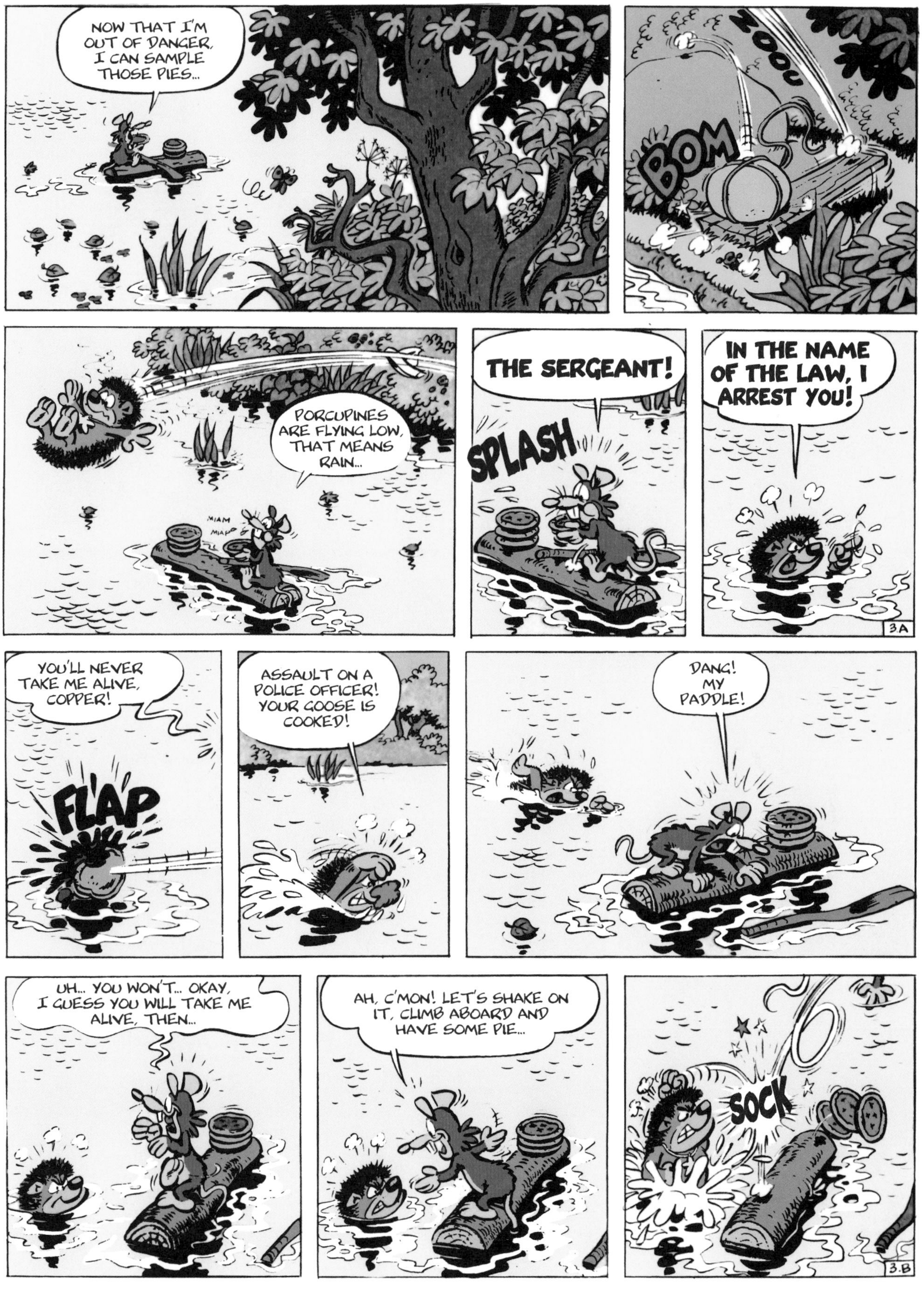

NOW THAT I'M OUT OF DANGER, I CAN SAMPLE THOSE PIES...
ZOOOU
BOM
PORCUPINES ARE FLYING LOW, THAT MEANS RAIN...
MIAM MIAM
THE SERGEANT!
SPLASH
IN THE NAME OF THE LAW, I ARREST YOU!
3A
YOU'LL NEVER TAKE ME ALIVE, COPPER!
FLAP
ASSAULT ON A POLICE OFFICER! YOUR GOOSE IS COOKED!
DANG! MY PADDLE!
UH... YOU WON'T... OKAY, I GUESS YOU WILL TAKE ME ALIVE, THEN...
AH, C'MON! LET'S SHAKE ON IT, CLIMB ABOARD AND HAVE SOME PIE...
SOCK
3.B

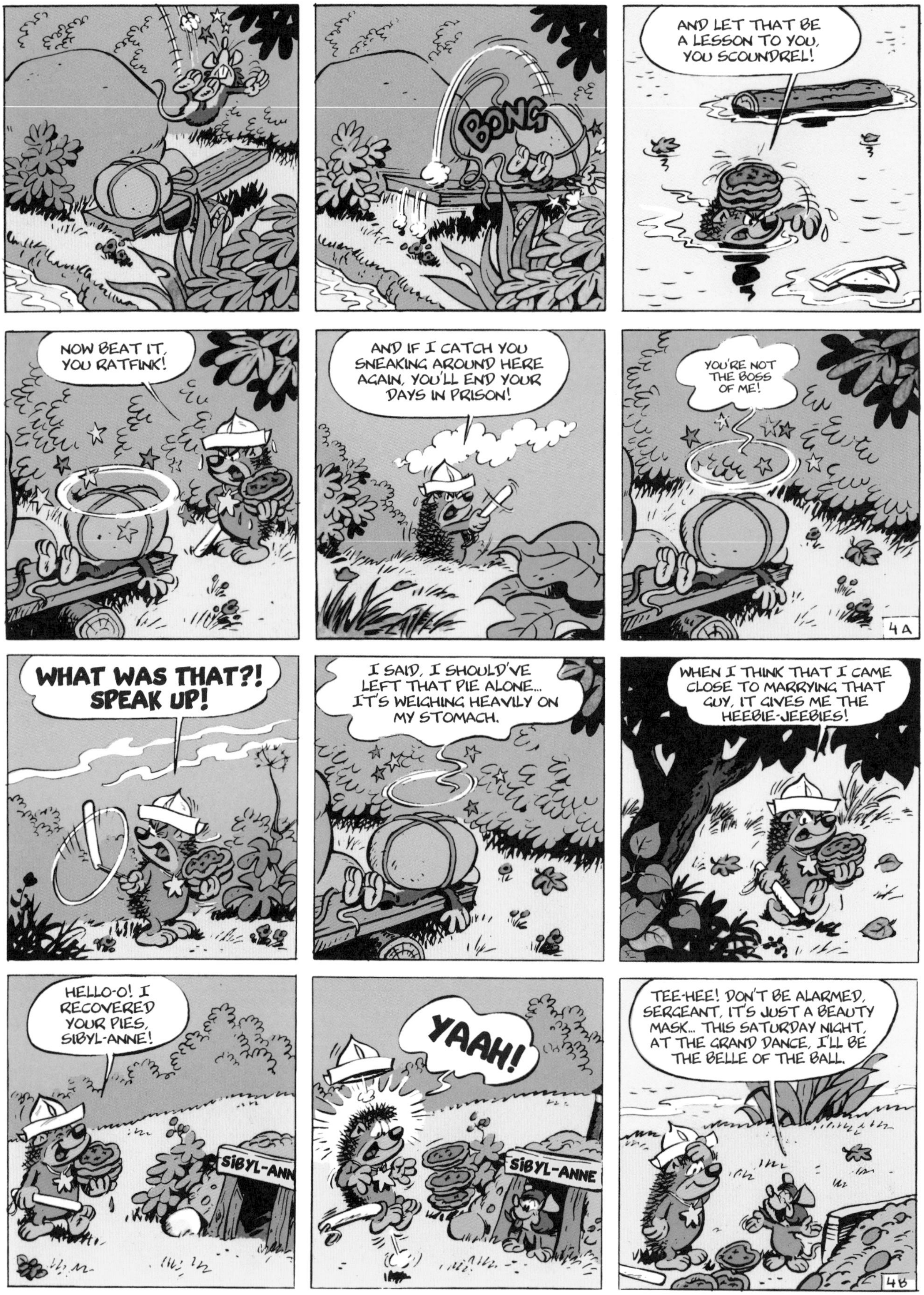
BONG
AND LET THAT BE A LESSON TO YOU, YOU SCOUNDREL!
NOW BEAT IT, YOU RATFINK!
AND IF I CATCH YOU SNEAKING AROUND HERE AGAIN, YOU'LL END YOUR DAYS IN PRISON!
YOU'RE NOT THE BOSS OF ME!
4A
WHAT WAS THAT?! SPEAK UP!
I SAID, I SHOULD'VE LEFT THAT PIE ALONE... IT'S WEIGHING HEAVILY ON MY STOMACH.
WHEN I THINK THAT I CAME CLOSE TO MARRYING THAT GUY, IT GIVES ME THE HEEBIE-JEEBIES!
HELLO-O! I RECOVERED YOUR PIES, SIBYL-ANNE!
SIBYL-ANNE
YAAH!
SIBYL-ANNE
TEE-HEE! DON'T BE ALARMED, SERGEANT, IT'S JUST A BEAUTY MASK... THIS SATURDAY NIGHT, AT THE GRAND DANCE, I'LL BE THE BELLE OF THE BALL.
4B

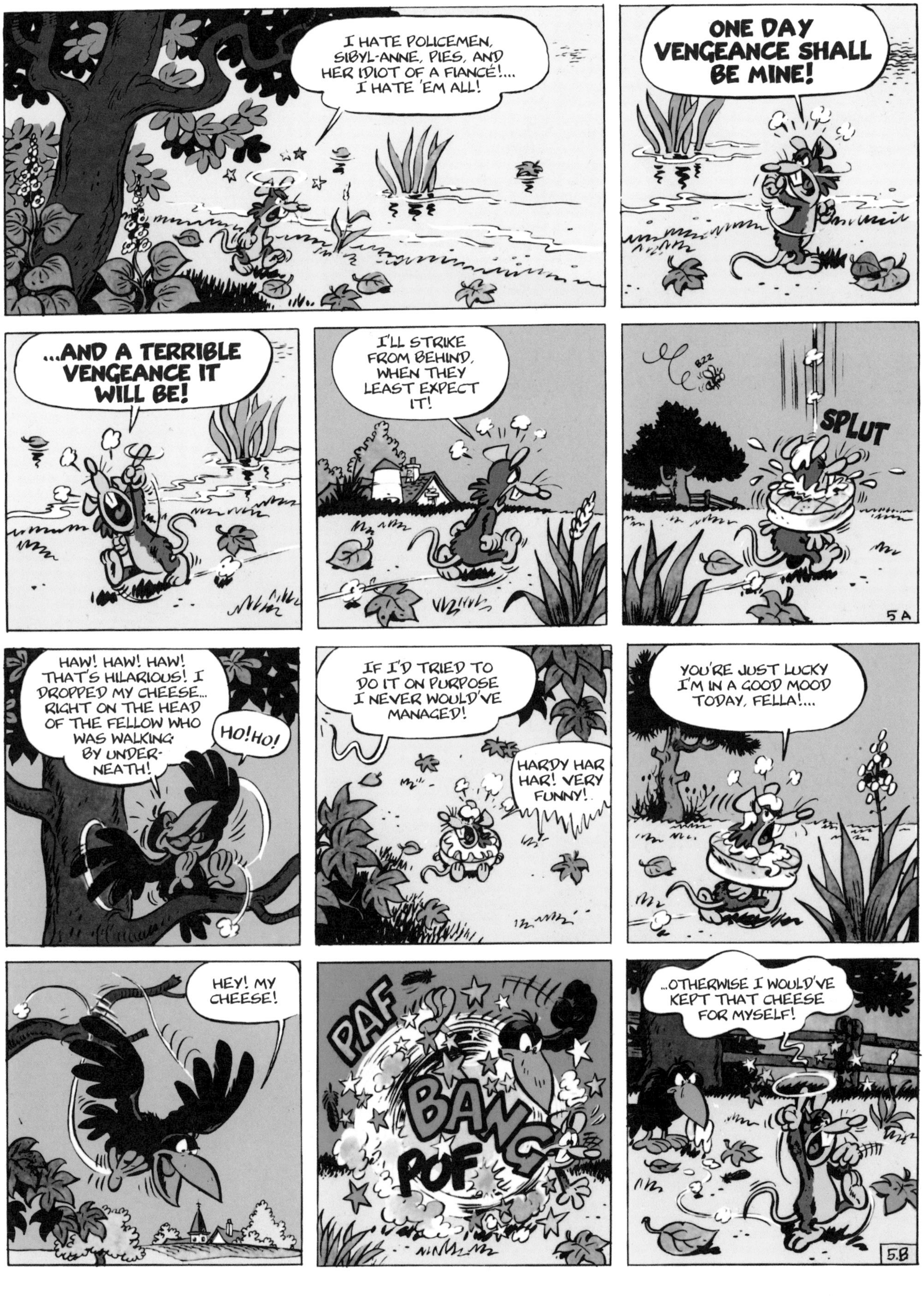
I HATE POLICEMEN, SIBYL-ANNE, PIES, AND HER IDIOT OF A FIANCÉ!... I HATE 'EM ALL!
ONE DAY VENGEANCE SHALL BE MINE!
...AND A TERRIBLE VENGEANCE IT WILL BE!
I'LL STRIKE FROM BEHIND, WHEN THEY LEAST EXPECT IT!
BZZ
SPLUT
5 A
HAW! HAW! HAW! THAT'S HILARIOUS! I DROPPED MY CHEESE... RIGHT ON THE HEAD OF THE FELLOW WHO WAS WALKING BY UNDER-NEATH!
HO! HO!
IF I'D TRIED TO DO IT ON PURPOSE I NEVER WOULD'VE MANAGED!
HARDY HAR HAR! VERY FUNNY!
YOU'RE JUST LUCKY I'M IN A GOOD MOOD TODAY, FELLA!...
HEY! MY CHEESE!
PAF
BANG
POF
...OTHERWISE I WOULD'VE KEPT THAT CHEESE FOR MYSELF!
5.B

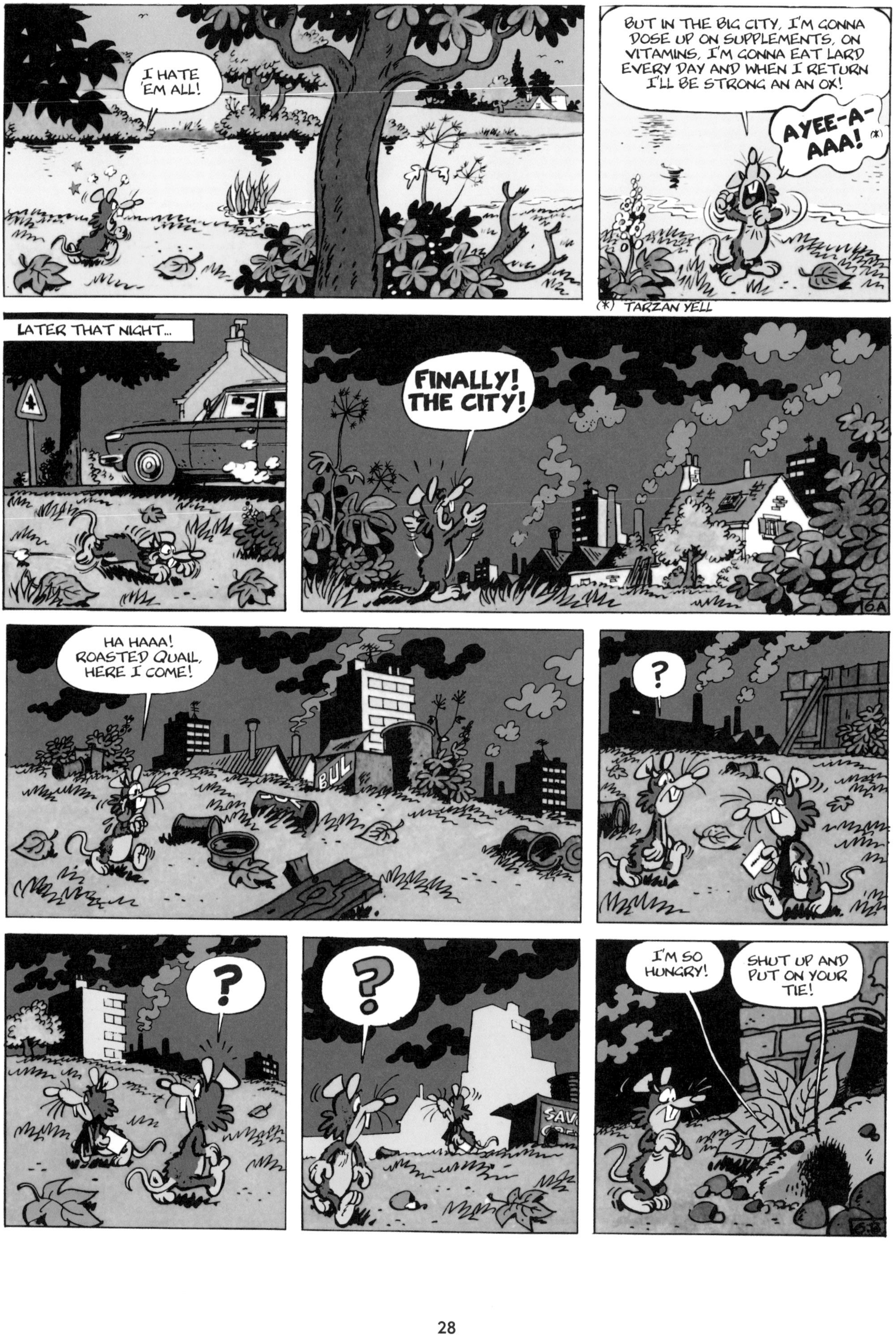
I HATE 'EM ALL!
BUT IN THE BIG CITY, I'M GONNA DOSE UP ON SUPPLEMENTS, ON VITAMINS, I'M GONNA EAT LARD EVERY DAY AND WHEN I RETURN I'LL BE STRONG AN AN OX!
AYEE-A-AAA! (*)
(*) TARZAN YELL
LATER THAT NIGHT...
FINALLY! THE CITY!
HA HAAA! ROASTED QUAIL, HERE I COME!
BUL
?
?
?
I'M SO HUNGRY!
SHUT UP AND PUT ON YOUR TIE!

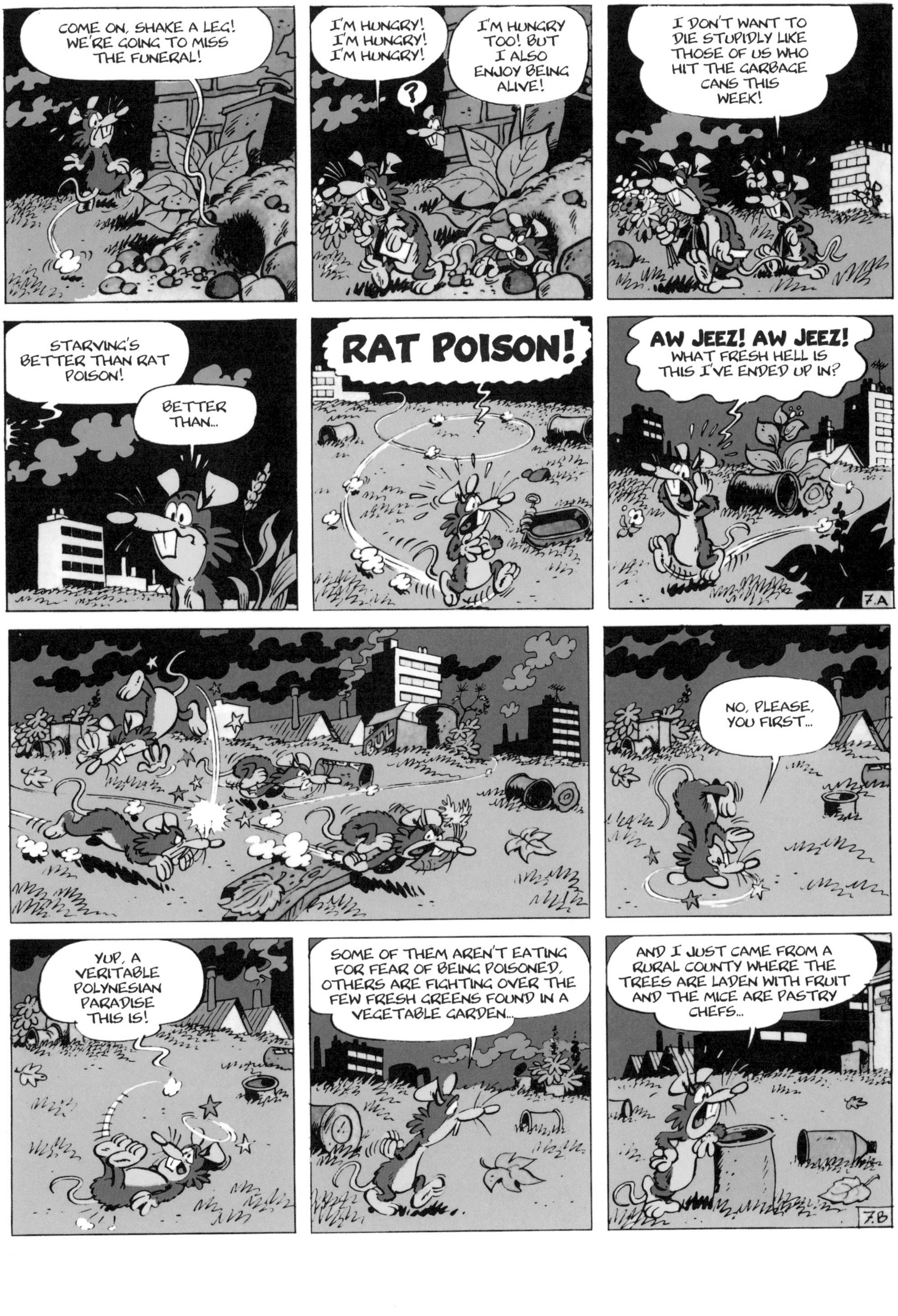
COME ON, SHAKE A LEG! WE'RE GOING TO MISS THE FUNERAL!
I'M HUNGRY! I'M HUNGRY! I'M HUNGRY!
?
I'M HUNGRY TOO! BUT I ALSO ENJOY BEING ALIVE!
I DON'T WANT TO DIE STUPIDLY LIKE THOSE OF US WHO HIT THE GARBAGE CANS THIS WEEK!
STARVING'S BETTER THAN RAT POISON!
BETTER THAN...
RAT POISON!
AW JEEZ! AW JEEZ! WHAT FRESH HELL IS THIS I'VE ENDED UP IN?
7.A
NO, PLEASE, YOU FIRST...
YUP, A VERITABLE POLYNESIAN PARADISE THIS IS!
SOME OF THEM AREN'T EATING FOR FEAR OF BEING POISONED, OTHERS ARE FIGHTING OVER THE FEW FRESH GREENS FOUND IN A VEGETABLE GARDEN...
AND I JUST CAME FROM A RURAL COUNTY WHERE THE TREES ARE LADEN WITH FRUIT AND THE MICE ARE PASTRY CHEFS...
7.B

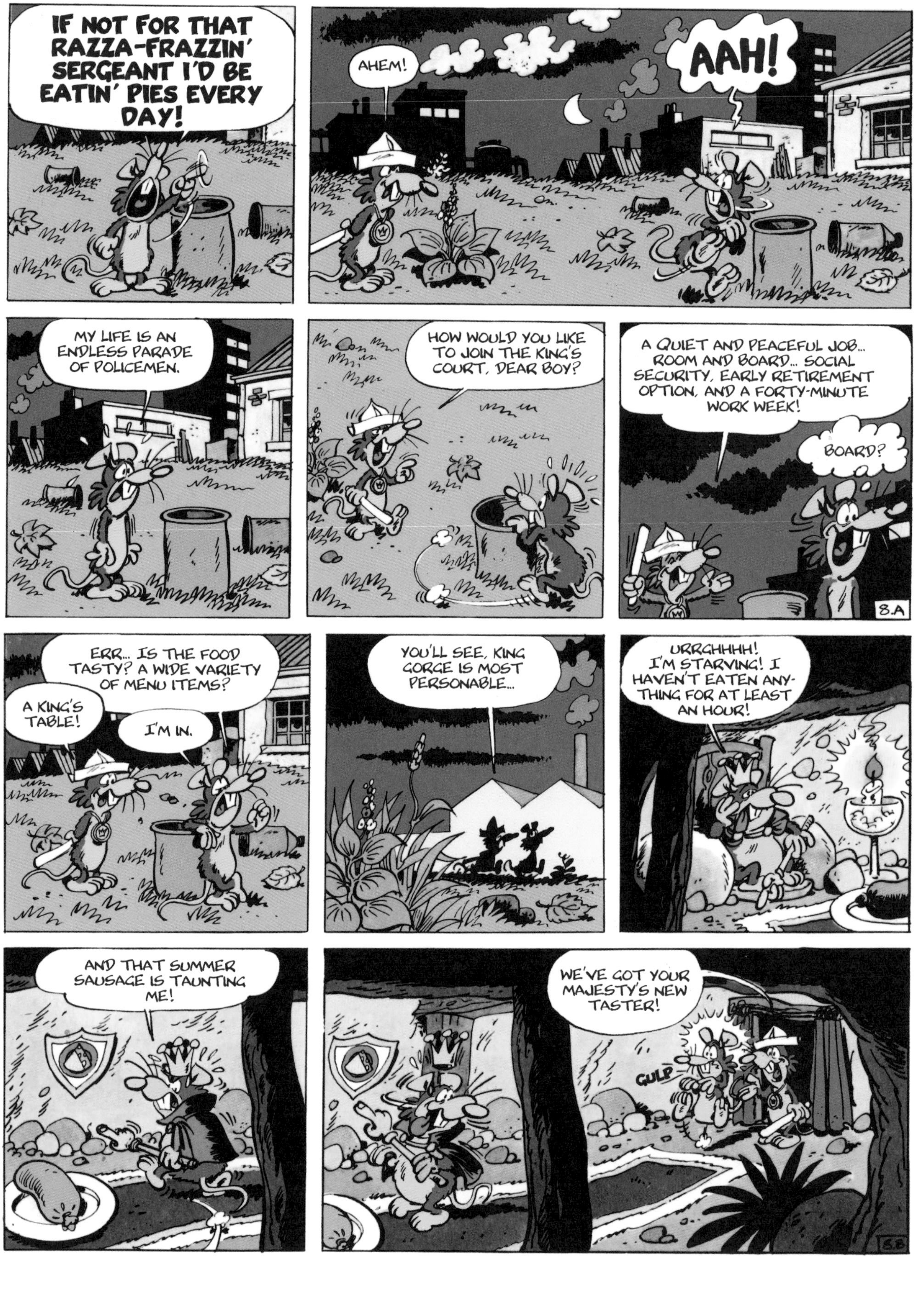
IF NOT FOR THAT RAZZA-FRAZZIN' SERGEANT I'D BE EATIN' PIES EVERY DAY!
AHEM!
AAH!
MY LIFE IS AN ENDLESS PARADE OF POLICEMEN.
HOW WOULD YOU LIKE TO JOIN THE KING'S COURT, DEAR BOY?
A QUIET AND PEACEFUL JOB... ROOM AND BOARD... SOCIAL SECURITY, EARLY RETIREMENT OPTION, AND A FORTY-MINUTE WORK WEEK!
BOARD?
8.A
ERR... IS THE FOOD TASTY? A WIDE VARIETY OF MENU ITEMS?
A KING'S TABLE!
I'M IN.
YOU'LL SEE, KING GORGE IS MOST PERSONABLE...
URRGHHHH! I'M STARVING! I HAVEN'T EATEN ANY-THING FOR AT LEAST AN HOUR!
AND THAT SUMMER SAUSAGE IS TAUNTING ME!
WE'VE GOT YOUR MAJESTY'S NEW TASTER!
GULP
8.B

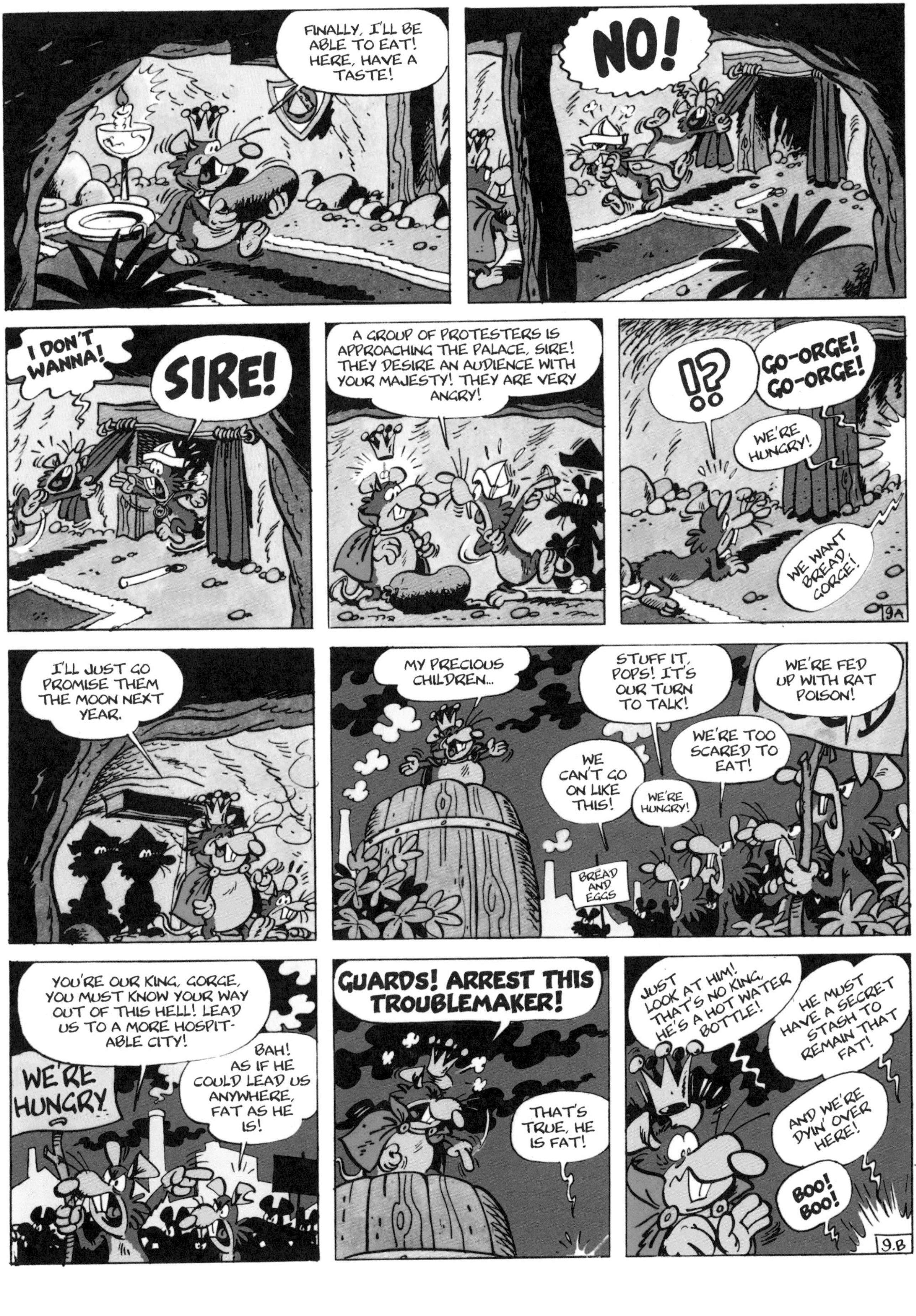

FINALLY, I'LL BE ABLE TO EAT! HERE, HAVE A TASTE!
NO!
I DON'T WANNA!
SIRE!
A GROUP OF PROTESTERS IS APPROACHING THE PALACE, SIRE! THEY DESIRE AN AUDIENCE WITH YOUR MAJESTY! THEY ARE VERY ANGRY!
!?
GO-ORGE! GO-ORGE!
WE'RE HUNGRY!
WE WANT BREAD, GORGE!
9A
I'LL JUST GO PROMISE THEM THE MOON NEXT YEAR.
MY PRECIOUS CHILDREN...
STUFF IT, POPS! IT'S OUR TURN TO TALK!
WE'RE FED UP WITH RAT POISON!
WE'RE TOO SCARED TO EAT!
WE CAN'T GO ON LIKE THIS!
WE'RE HUNGRY!
BREAD AND EGGS
YOU'RE OUR KING, GORGE, YOU MUST KNOW YOUR WAY OUT OF THIS HELL! LEAD US TO A MORE HOSPIT-ABLE CITY!
WE'RE HUNGRY
BAH! AS IF HE COULD LEAD US ANYWHERE, FAT AS HE IS!
GUARDS! ARREST THIS TROUBLEMAKER!
THAT'S TRUE, HE IS FAT!
JUST LOOK AT HIM! THAT'S NO KING, HE'S A HOT WATER BOTTLE!
HE MUST HAVE A SECRET STASH TO REMAIN THAT FAT!
AND WE'RE DYIN' OVER HERE!
BOO! BOO!
9.B

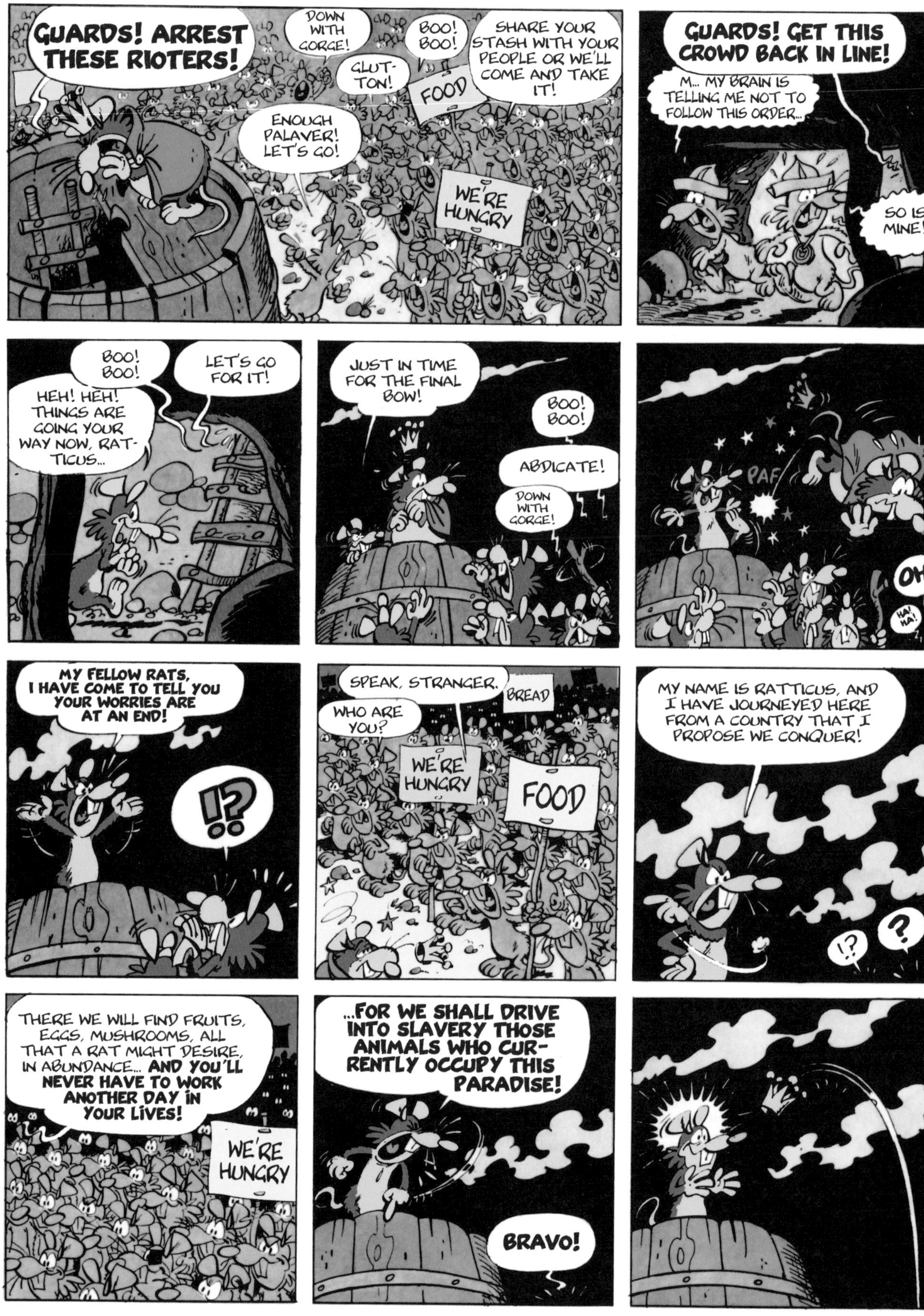
GUARDS! ARREST THESE RIOTERS!
DOWN WITH GORGE!
BOO! BOO!
SHARE YOUR STASH WITH YOUR PEOPLE OR WE'LL COME AND TAKE IT!
GLUT-TON!
FOOD
ENOUGH PALAVER! LET'S GO!
WE'RE HUNGRY
GUARDS! GET THIS CROWD BACK IN LINE!
M... MY BRAIN IS TELLING ME NOT TO FOLLOW THIS ORDER...
SO IS MINE!
BOO! BOO!
LET'S GO FOR IT!
HEH! HEH! THINGS ARE GOING YOUR WAY NOW, RAT-TICUS...
JUST IN TIME FOR THE FINAL BOW!
BOO! BOO!
ABDICATE!
DOWN WITH GORGE!
PAF
OH!
HA! HA!
MY FELLOW RATS, I HAVE COME TO TELL YOU YOUR WORRIES ARE AT AN END!
!?
SPEAK, STRANGER.
BREAD
WHO ARE YOU?
WE'RE HUNGRY
FOOD
MY NAME IS RATTICUS, AND I HAVE JOURNEYED HERE FROM A COUNTRY THAT I PROPOSE WE CONQUER!
!?
?
THERE WE WILL FIND FRUITS, EGGS, MUSHROOMS, ALL THAT A RAT MIGHT DESIRE, IN ABUNDANCE... AND YOU'LL NEVER HAVE TO WORK ANOTHER DAY IN YOUR LIVES!
WE'RE HUNGRY
...FOR WE SHALL DRIVE INTO SLAVERY THOSE ANIMALS WHO CUR-RENTLY OCCUPY THIS PARADISE!
BRAVO!

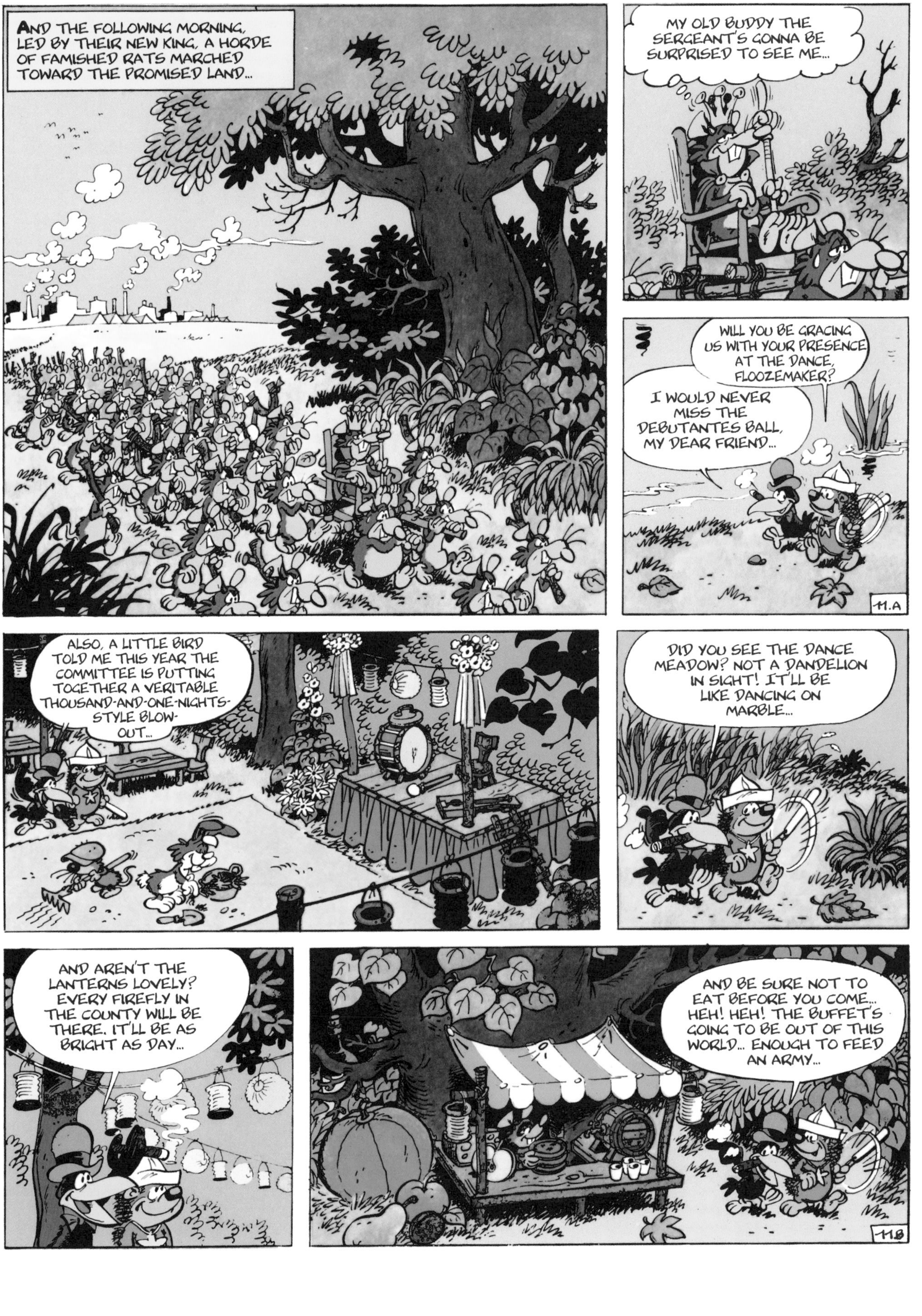
AND THE FOLLOWING MORNING, LED BY THEIR NEW KING, A HORDE OF FAMISHED RATS MARCHED TOWARD THE PROMISED LAND...
MY OLD BUDDY THE SERGEANT'S GONNA BE SURPRISED TO SEE ME...
WILL YOU BE GRACING US WITH YOUR PRESENCE AT THE DANCE, FLOOZEMAKER?
I WOULD NEVER MISS THE DEBUTANTES BALL, MY DEAR FRIEND...
11.A
ALSO, A LITTLE BIRD TOLD ME THIS YEAR THE COMMITTEE IS PUTTING TOGETHER A VERITABLE THOUSAND-AND-ONE-NIGHTS-STYLE BLOW-OUT...
DID YOU SEE THE DANCE MEADOW? NOT A DANDELION IN SIGHT! IT'LL BE LIKE DANCING ON MARBLE...
AND AREN'T THE LANTERNS LOVELY? EVERY FIREFLY IN THE COUNTY WILL BE THERE. IT'LL BE AS BRIGHT AS DAY...
AND BE SURE NOT TO EAT BEFORE YOU COME... HEH! HEH! THE BUFFET'S GOING TO BE OUT OF THIS WORLD... ENOUGH TO FEED AN ARMY...
11.B

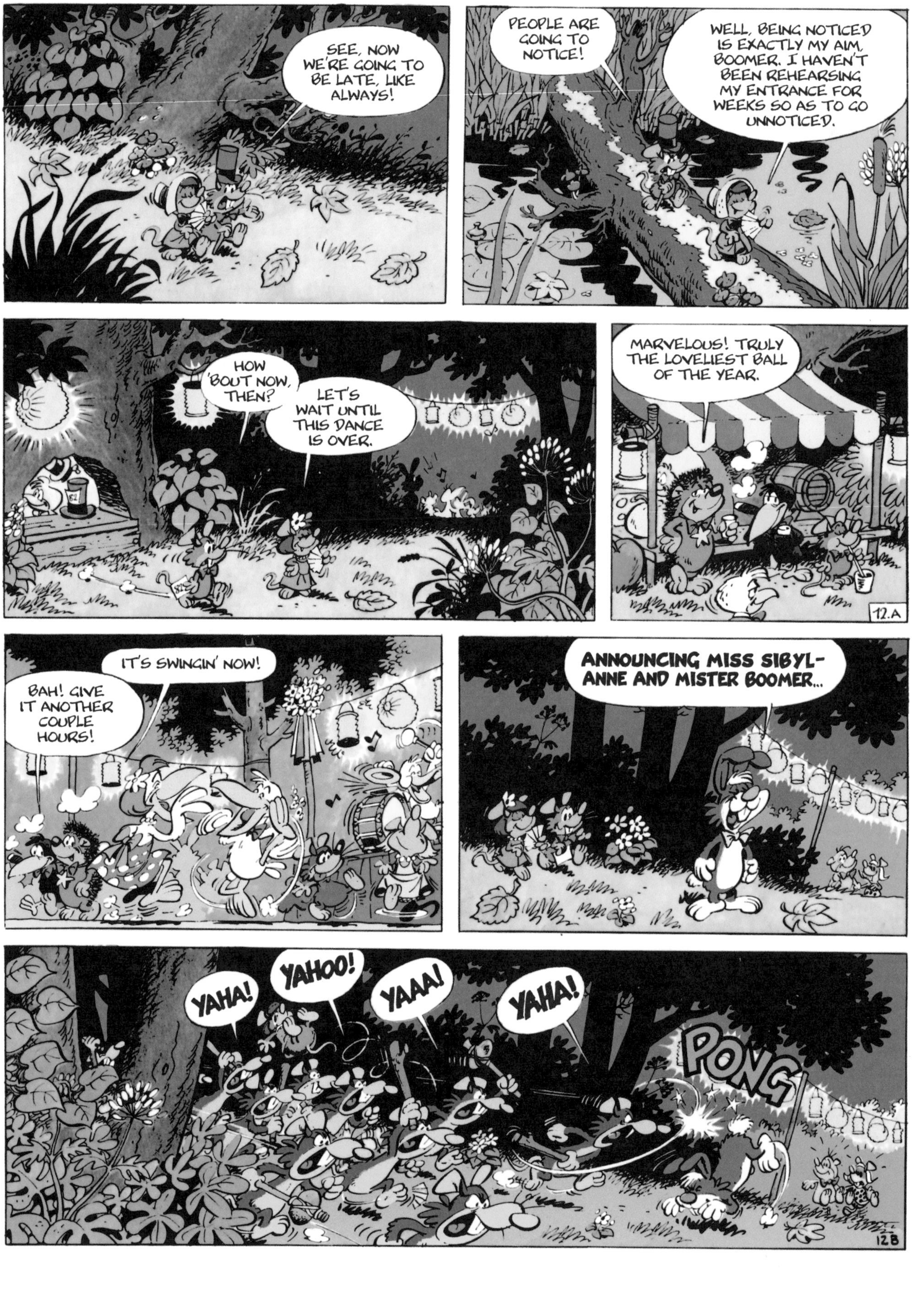
SEE, NOW WE'RE GOING TO BE LATE, LIKE ALWAYS!
PEOPLE ARE GOING TO NOTICE!
WELL, BEING NOTICED IS EXACTLY MY AIM, BOOMER. I HAVEN'T BEEN REHEARSING MY ENTRANCE FOR WEEKS SO AS TO GO UNNOTICED.
HOW 'BOUT NOW, THEN?
LET'S WAIT UNTIL THIS DANCE IS OVER.
MARVELOUS! TRULY THE LOVELIEST BALL OF THE YEAR.
12.A
IT'S SWINGIN' NOW!
BAH! GIVE IT ANOTHER COUPLE HOURS!
ANNOUNCING MISS SIBYL-ANNE AND MISTER BOOMER...
YAHA!
YAHOO!
YAAA!
YAHA!
PONG
12B

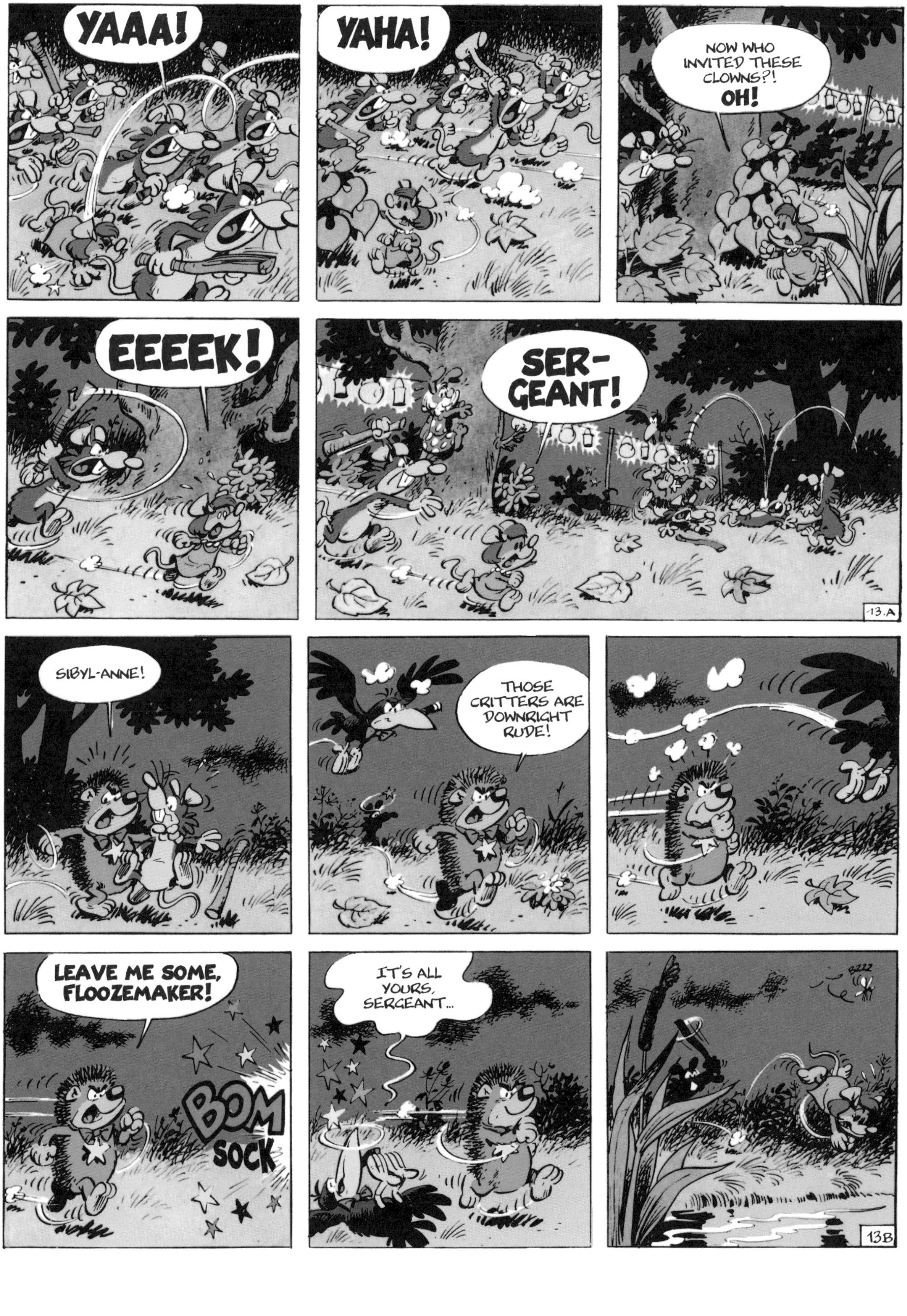
YAAA!
YAHA!
NOW WHO INVITED THESE CLOWNS?! OH!
EEEEK!
SER-GEANT!
13.A
SIBYL-ANNE!
THOSE CRITTERS ARE DOWNRIGHT RUDE!
LEAVE ME SOME, FLOOZEMAKER!
BOM
SOCK
IT'S ALL YOURS, SERGEANT...
BZZZ
13B

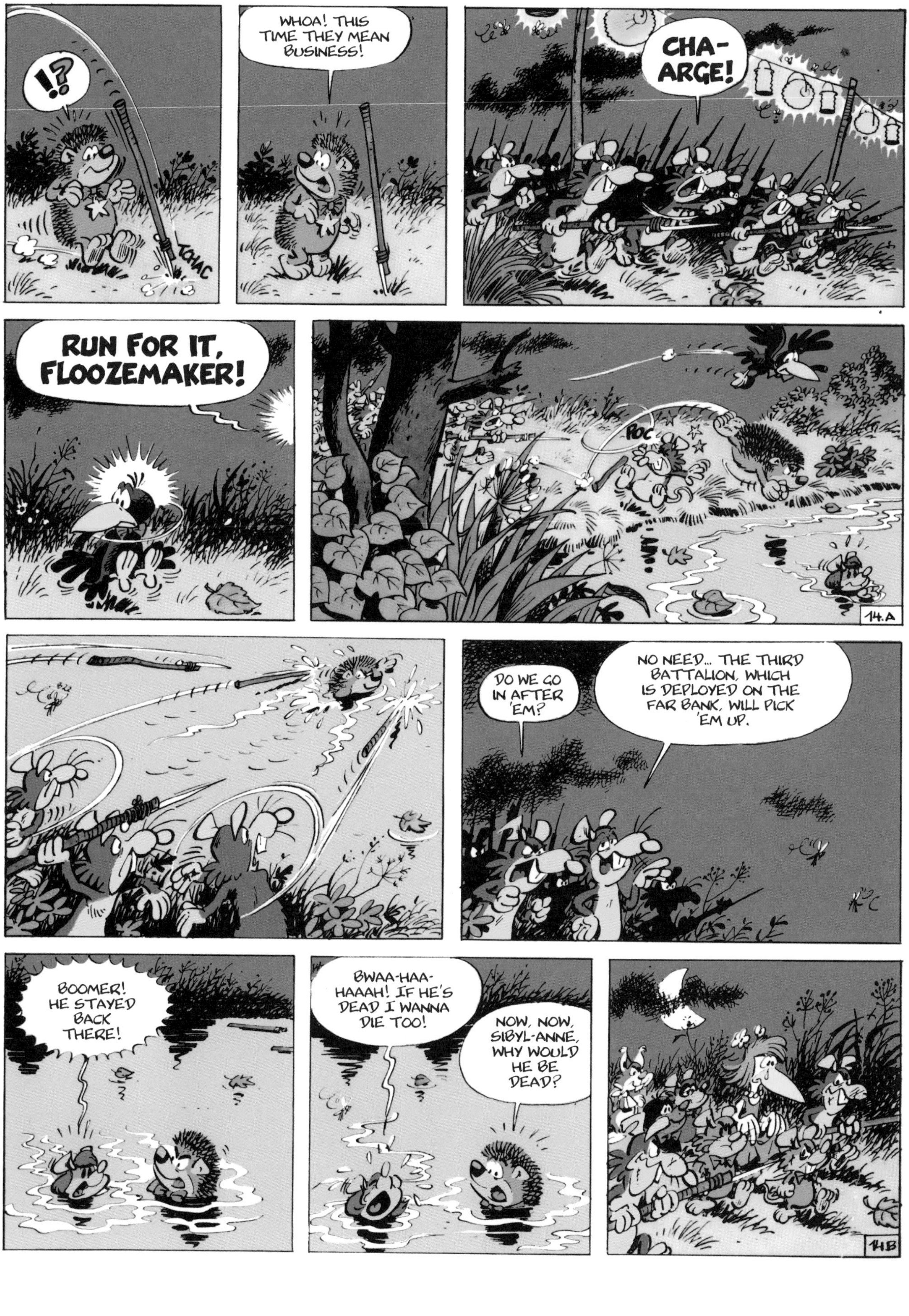
!?
TCHAC
WHOA! THIS TIME THEY MEAN BUSINESS!
CHA-ARGE!
RUN FOR IT, FLOOZEMAKER!
POC
14.A
DO WE GO IN AFTER 'EM?
NO NEED... THE THIRD BATTALION, WHICH IS DEPLOYED ON THE FAR BANK, WILL PICK 'EM UP.
BOOMER! HE STAYED BACK THERE!
BWAA-HAA-HAAAH! IF HE'S DEAD I WANNA DIE TOO!
NOW, NOW, SIBYL-ANNE, WHY WOULD HE BE DEAD?
14.B

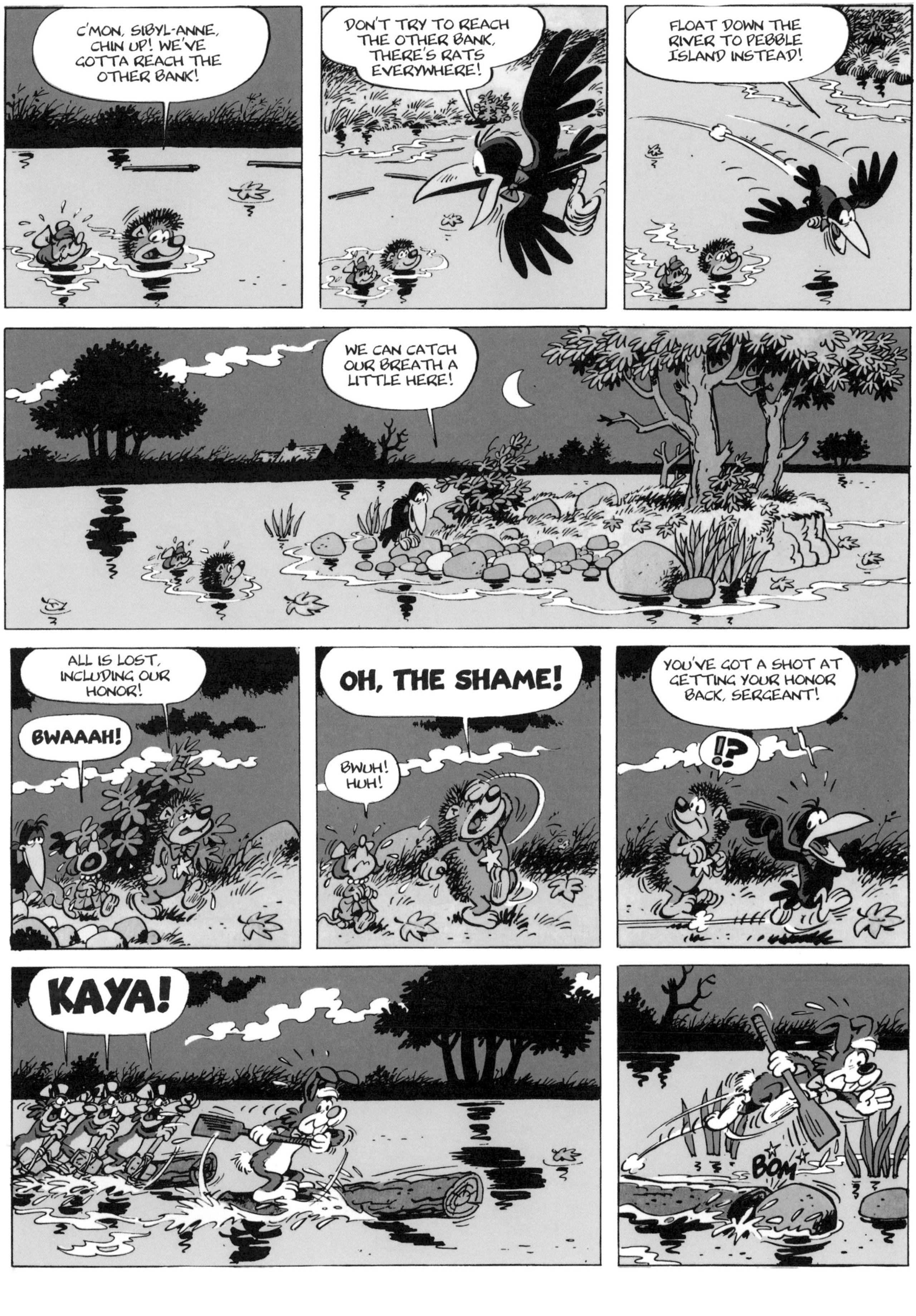
C'MON, SIBYL-ANNE, CHIN UP! WE'VE GOTTA REACH THE OTHER BANK!
DON'T TRY TO REACH THE OTHER BANK, THERE'S RATS EVERYWHERE!
FLOAT DOWN THE RIVER TO PEBBLE ISLAND INSTEAD!
WE CAN CATCH OUR BREATH A LITTLE HERE!
ALL IS LOST, INCLUDING OUR HONOR!
BWAAAH!
OH, THE SHAME!
BWUH! HUH!
YOU'VE GOT A SHOT AT GETTING YOUR HONOR BACK, SERGEANT!
!?
KAYA!
BOM

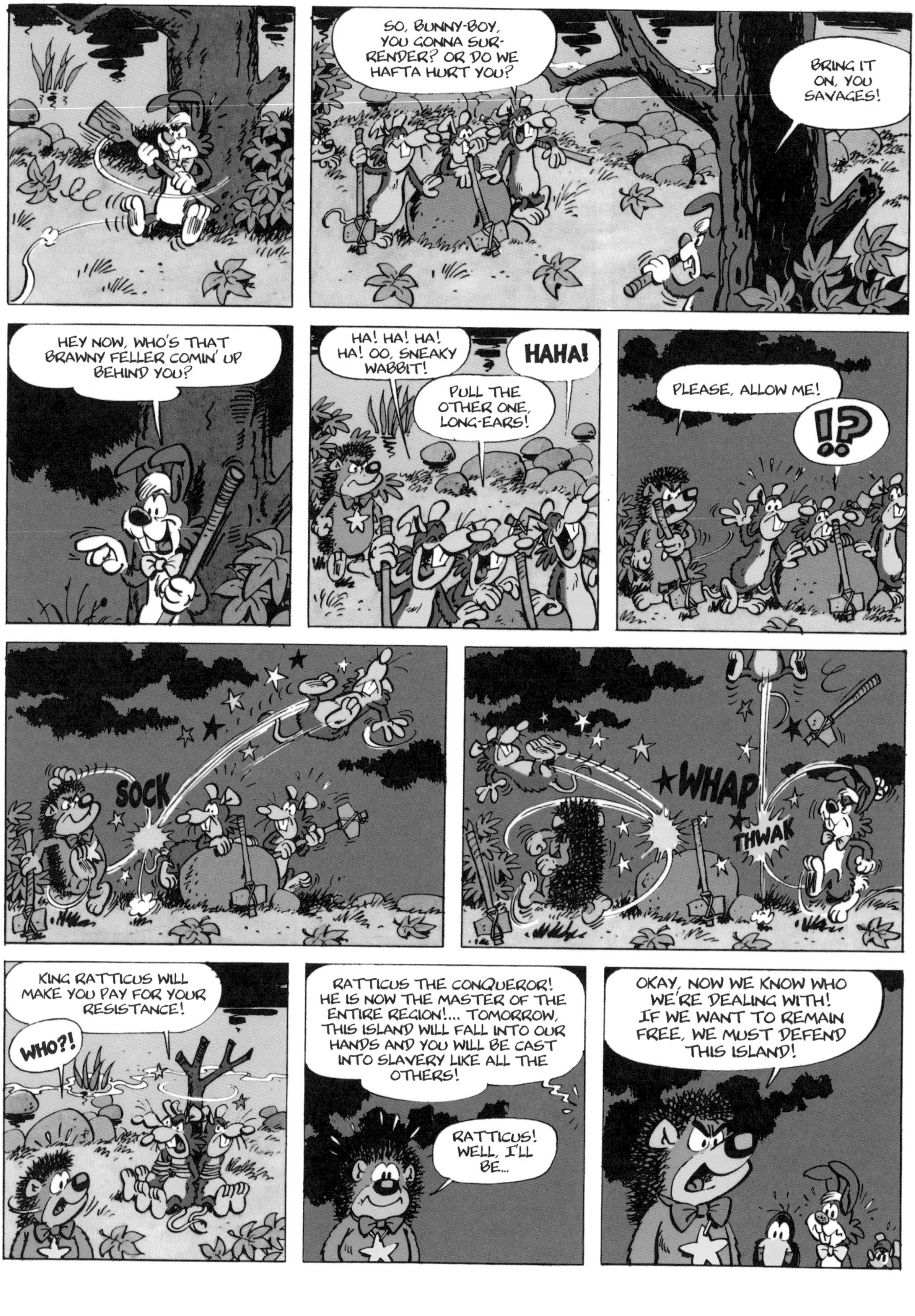
SO, BUNNY-BOY, YOU GONNA SUR-RENDER? OR DO WE HAFTA HURT YOU?
BRING IT ON, YOU SAVAGES!
HEY NOW, WHO'S THAT BRAWNY FELLER COMIN' UP BEHIND YOU?
HA! HA! HA! HA! OO, SNEAKY WABBIT!
HAHA!
PULL THE OTHER ONE, LONG-EARS!
PLEASE, ALLOW ME!
!?
SOCK
WHAP
THWAK
KING RATTICUS WILL MAKE YOU PAY FOR YOUR RESISTANCE!
WHO?!
RATTICUS THE CONQUEROR! HE IS NOW THE MASTER OF THE ENTIRE REGION!... TOMORROW, THIS ISLAND WILL FALL INTO OUR HANDS AND YOU WILL BE CAST INTO SLAVERY LIKE ALL THE OTHERS!
RATTICUS! WELL, I'LL BE...
OKAY, NOW WE KNOW WHO WE'RE DEALING WITH! IF WE WANT TO REMAIN FREE, WE MUST DEFEND THIS ISLAND!

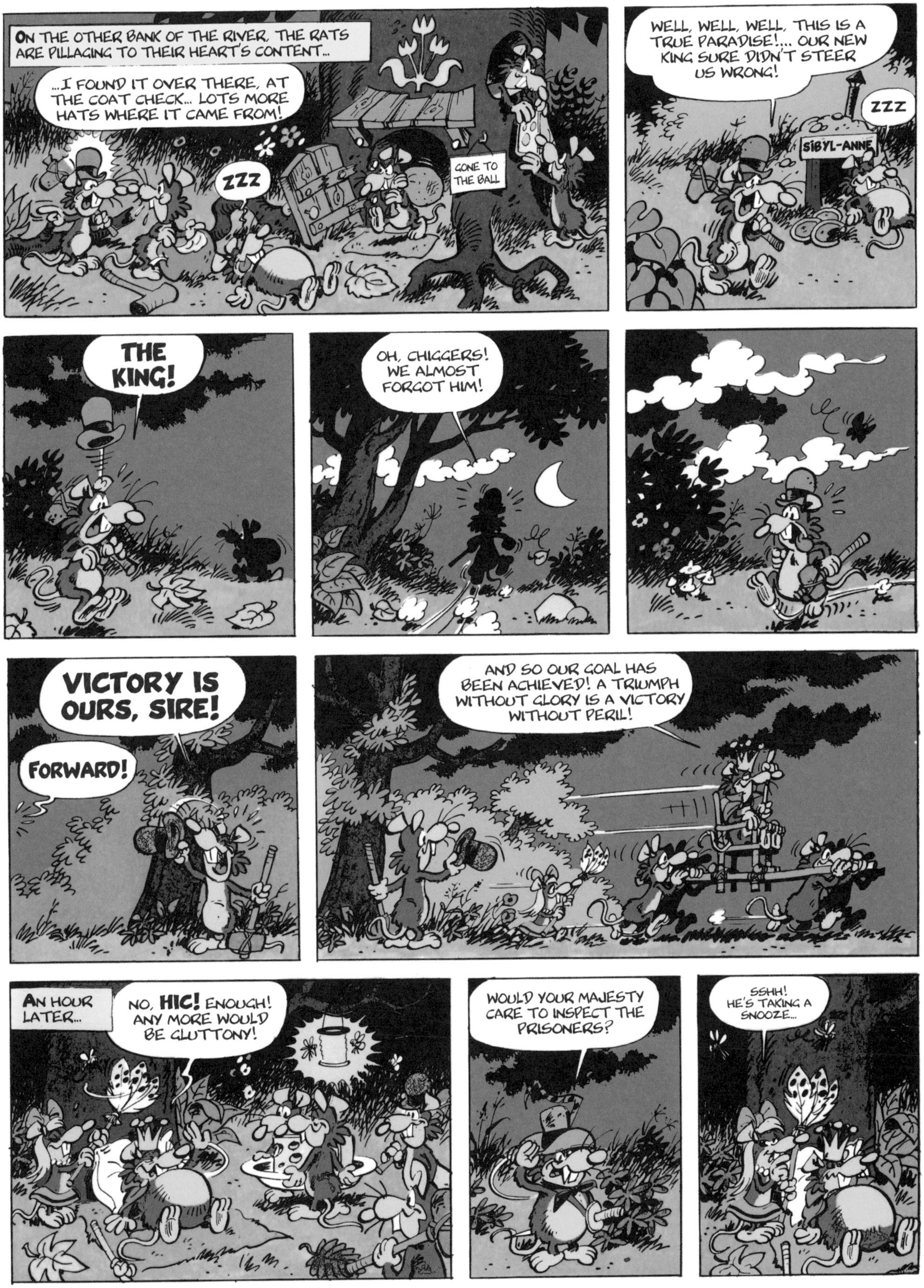

ON THE OTHER BANK OF THE RIVER, THE RATS ARE PILLAGING TO THEIR HEART'S CONTENT...
...I FOUND IT OVER THERE, AT THE COAT CHECK... LOTS MORE HATS WHERE IT CAME FROM!
ZZZ
GONE TO THE BALL
WELL, WELL, WELL, THIS IS A TRUE PARADISE!... OUR NEW KING SURE DIDN'T STEER US WRONG!
ZZZ
SIBYL-ANNE
THE KING!
OH, CHIGGERS! WE ALMOST FORGOT HIM!
VICTORY IS OURS, SIRE!
FORWARD!
AND SO OUR GOAL HAS BEEN ACHIEVED! A TRIUMPH WITHOUT GLORY IS A VICTORY WITHOUT PERIL!
AN HOUR LATER...
NO, HIC! ENOUGH! ANY MORE WOULD BE GLUTTONY!
WOULD YOUR MAJESTY CARE TO INSPECT THE PRISONERS?
SSHH! HE'S TAKING A SNOOZE...

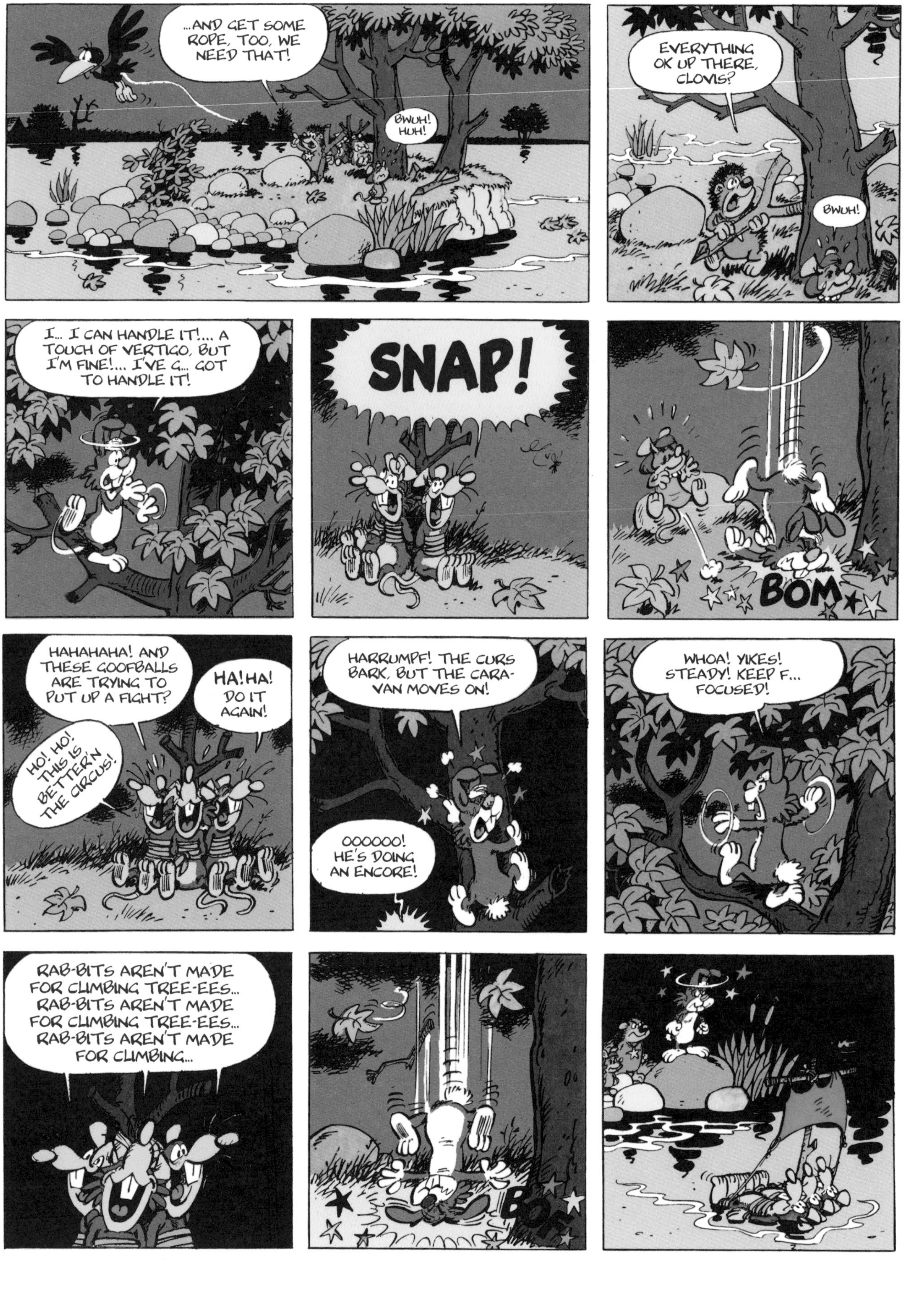
...AND GET SOME ROPE, TOO, WE NEED THAT!
BWUH! HUH!
EVERYTHING OK UP THERE, CLOVIS?
BWUH!
I... I CAN HANDLE IT!... A TOUCH OF VERTIGO, BUT I'M FINE!... I'VE G... GOT TO HANDLE IT!
SNAP!
BOM
HAHAHAHA! AND THESE GOOFBALLS ARE TRYING TO PUT UP A FIGHT?
HA! HA! DO IT AGAIN!
HO! HO! THIS IS BETTER'N THE CIRCUS!
HARRUMPF! THE CURS BARK, BUT THE CARA-VAN MOVES ON!
OOOOOO! HE'S DOING AN ENCORE!
WHOA! YIKES! STEADY! KEEP F... FOCUSED!
RAB-BITS AREN'T MADE FOR CLIMBING TREE-EES... RAB-BITS AREN'T MADE FOR CLIMBING TREE-EES... RAB-BITS AREN'T MADE FOR CLIMBING...
BOF

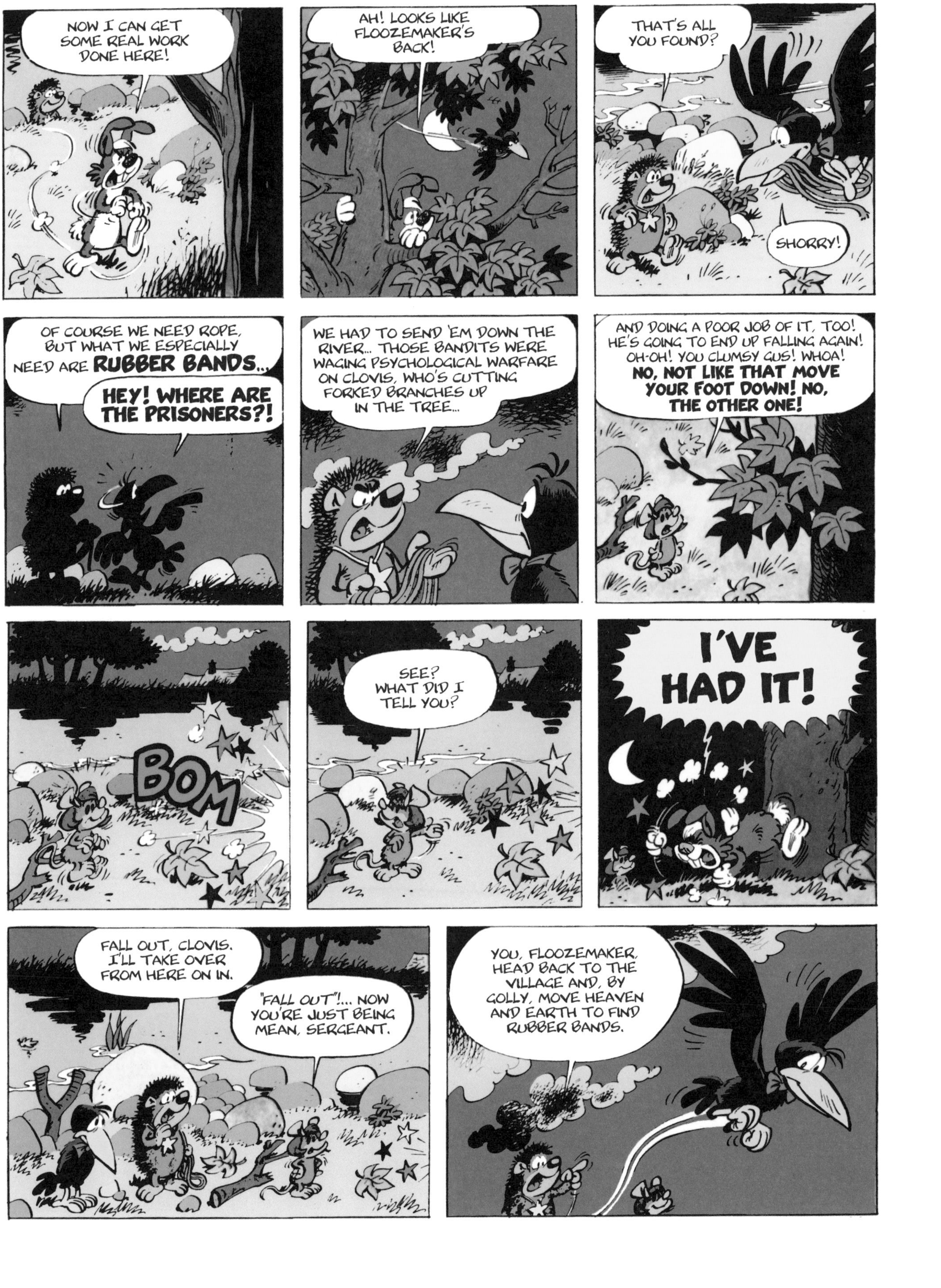

NOW I CAN GET SOME REAL WORK DONE HERE!
AH! LOOKS LIKE FLOOZEMAKER'S BACK!
THAT'S ALL YOU FOUND?
SHORRY!
OF COURSE WE NEED ROPE, BUT WHAT WE ESPECIALLY NEED ARE **RUBBER BANDS**...
**HEY! WHERE ARE THE PRISONERS?!**
WE HAD TO SEND 'EM DOWN THE RIVER... THOSE BANDITS WERE WAGING PSYCHOLOGICAL WARFARE ON CLOVIS, WHO'S CUTTING FORKED BRANCHES UP IN THE TREE...
AND DOING A POOR JOB OF IT, TOO! HE'S GOING TO END UP FALLING AGAIN! OH-OH! YOU CLUMSY GUS! WHOA! **NO, NOT LIKE THAT MOVE YOUR FOOT DOWN! NO, THE OTHER ONE!**
BOM
SEE? WHAT DID I TELL YOU?
I'VE HAD IT!
FALL OUT, CLOVIS. I'LL TAKE OVER FROM HERE ON IN.
"FALL OUT"!... NOW YOU'RE JUST BEING MEAN, SERGEANT.
YOU, FLOOZEMAKER, HEAD BACK TO THE VILLAGE AND, BY GOLLY, MOVE HEAVEN AND EARTH TO FIND RUBBER BANDS.

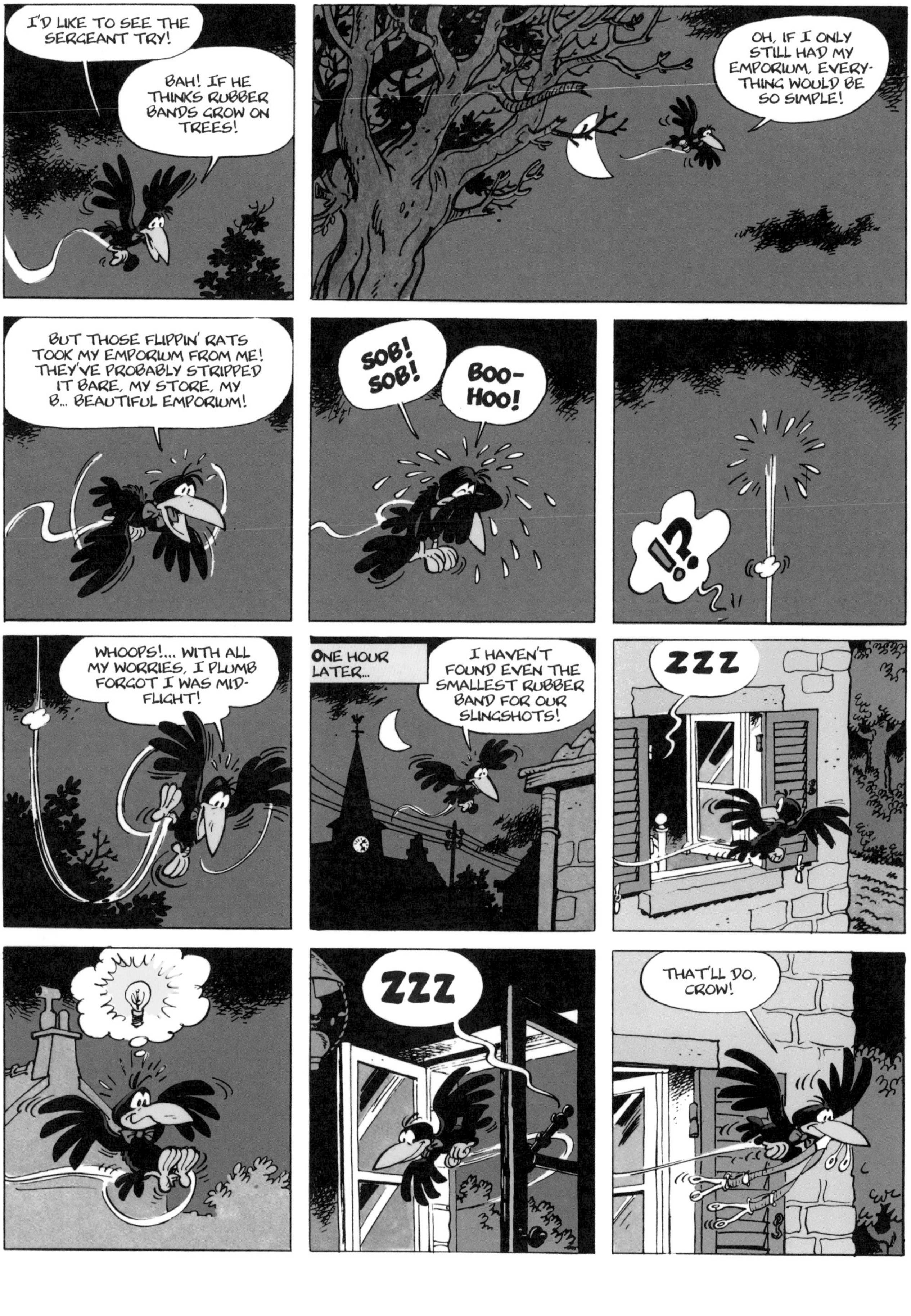

I'D LIKE TO SEE THE SERGEANT TRY!
BAH! IF HE THINKS RUBBER BANDS GROW ON TREES!
OH, IF I ONLY STILL HAD MY EMPORIUM, EVERY-THING WOULD BE SO SIMPLE!
BUT THOSE FLIPPIN' RATS TOOK MY EMPORIUM FROM ME! THEY'VE PROBABLY STRIPPED IT BARE, MY STORE, MY B... BEAUTIFUL EMPORIUM!
SOB! SOB!
BOO-HOO!
!?
WHOOPS!... WITH ALL MY WORRIES, I PLUMB FORGOT I WAS MID-FLIGHT!
ONE HOUR LATER...
I HAVEN'T FOUND EVEN THE SMALLEST RUBBER BAND FOR OUR SLINGSHOTS!
ZZZ
ZZZ
THAT'LL DO, CROW!

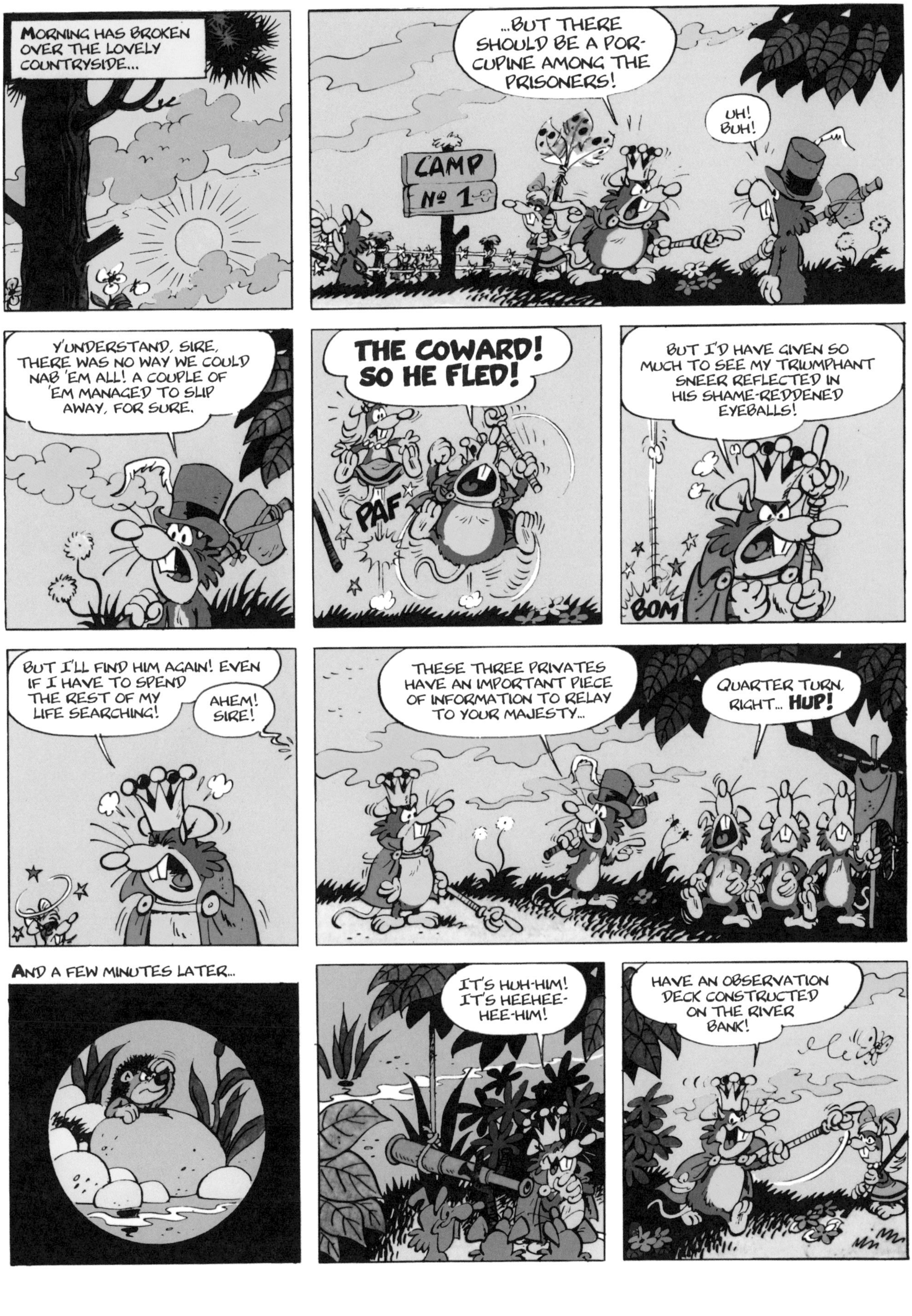
MORNING HAS BROKEN OVER THE LOVELY COUNTRYSIDE...
...BUT THERE SHOULD BE A PORCUPINE AMONG THE PRISONERS!
CAMP Nº 1
UH! BUH!
Y'UNDERSTAND, SIRE, THERE WAS NO WAY WE COULD NAB 'EM ALL! A COUPLE OF 'EM MANAGED TO SLIP AWAY, FOR SURE.
THE COWARD! SO HE FLED!
PAF
BUT I'D HAVE GIVEN SO MUCH TO SEE MY TRIUMPHANT SNEER REFLECTED IN HIS SHAME-REDDENED EYEBALLS!
BOM
BUT I'LL FIND HIM AGAIN! EVEN IF I HAVE TO SPEND THE REST OF MY LIFE SEARCHING!
AHEM! SIRE!
THESE THREE PRIVATES HAVE AN IMPORTANT PIECE OF INFORMATION TO RELAY TO YOUR MAJESTY...
QUARTER TURN, RIGHT... HUP!
AND A FEW MINUTES LATER...
IT'S HUH-HIM! IT'S HEEHEE-HEE-HIM!
HAVE AN OBSERVATION DECK CONSTRUCTED ON THE RIVER BANK!

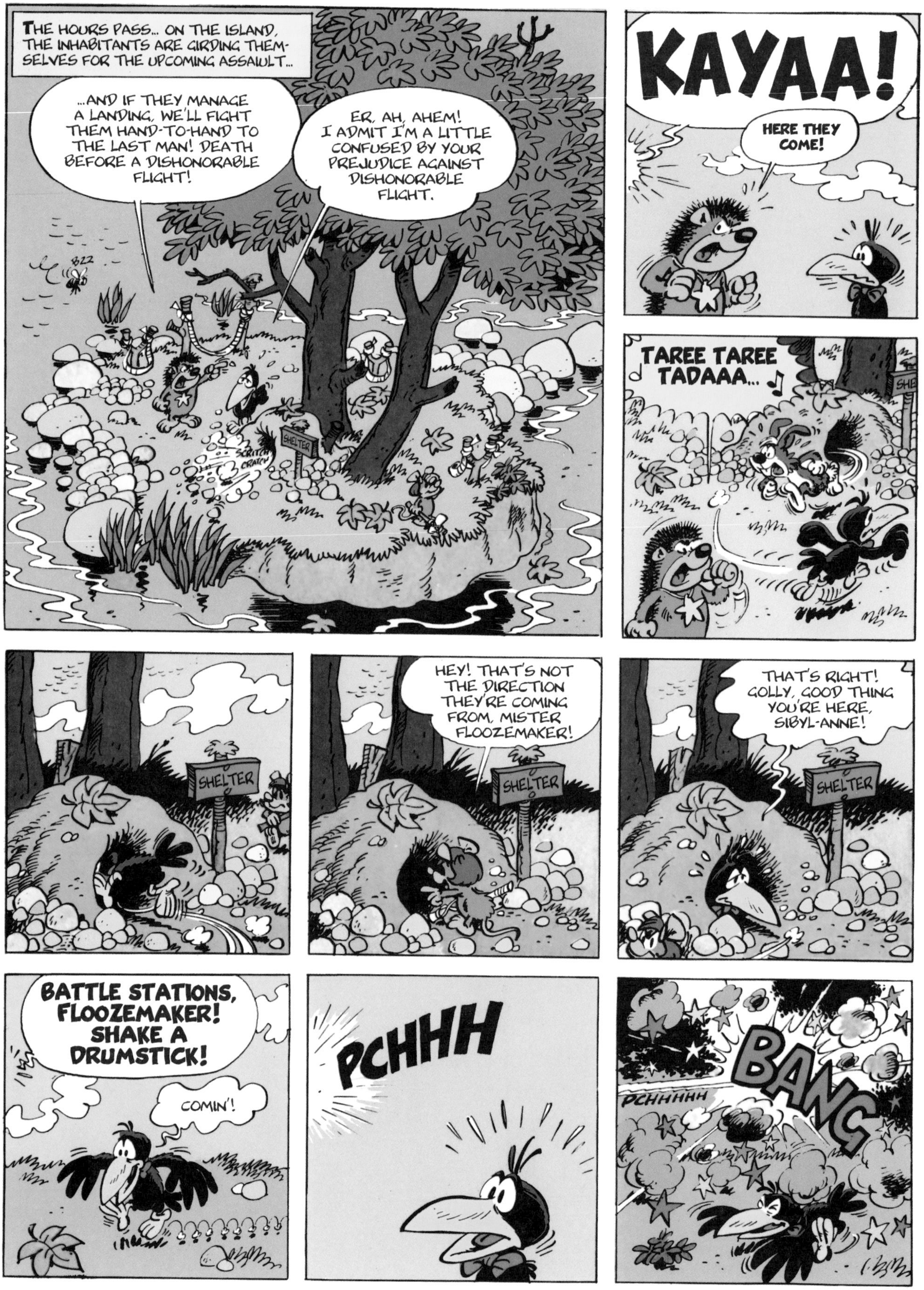
THE HOURS PASS... ON THE ISLAND, THE INHABITANTS ARE GIRDING THEMSELVES FOR THE UPCOMING ASSAULT...
...AND IF THEY MANAGE A LANDING, WE'LL FIGHT THEM HAND-TO-HAND TO THE LAST MAN! DEATH BEFORE A DISHONORABLE FLIGHT!
ER, AH, AHEM! I ADMIT I'M A LITTLE CONFUSED BY YOUR PREJUDICE AGAINST DISHONORABLE FLIGHT.
BZZ
SHELTER
SCRATCH SCRATCH
KAYAA!
HERE THEY COME!
TAREE TAREE TADAAA...
SHELTER
HEY! THAT'S NOT THE DIRECTION THEY'RE COMING FROM, MISTER FLOOZEMAKER!
SHELTER
THAT'S RIGHT! GOLLY, GOOD THING YOU'RE HERE, SIBYL-ANNE!
SHELTER
BATTLE STATIONS, FLOOZEMAKER! SHAKE A DRUMSTICK!
COMIN'!
PCHHH
PCHHHHH
BANG

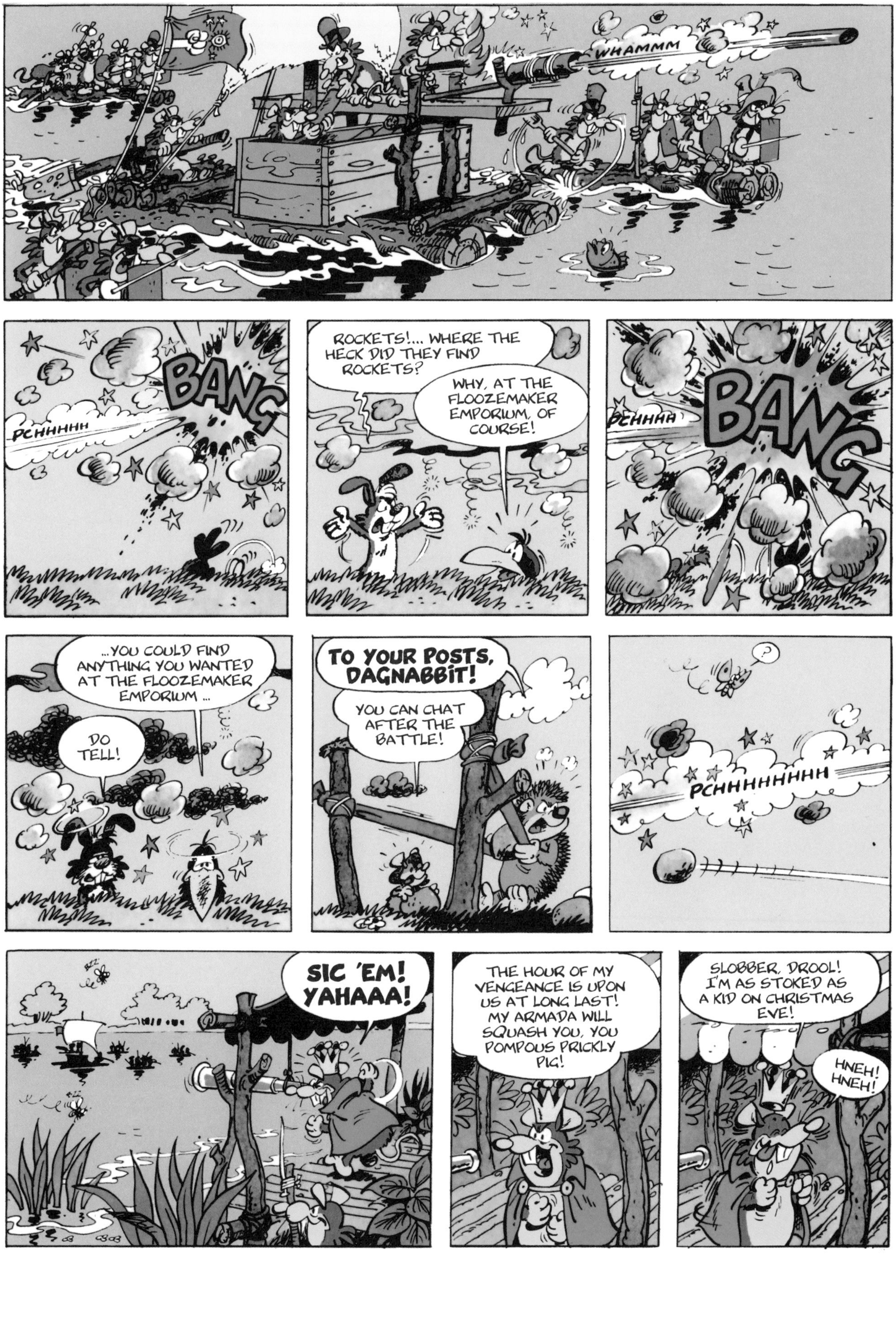
WHAMMM
PCHHHHH
BANG
ROCKETS!... WHERE THE HECK DID THEY FIND ROCKETS?
WHY, AT THE FLOOZEMAKER EMPORIUM, OF COURSE!
PCHHHH
BANG
...YOU COULD FIND ANYTHING YOU WANTED AT THE FLOOZEMAKER EMPORIUM ...
DO TELL!
TO YOUR POSTS, DAGNABBIT!
YOU CAN CHAT AFTER THE BATTLE!
?
PCHHHHHHHH
SIC 'EM! YAHAAA!
THE HOUR OF MY VENGEANCE IS UPON US AT LONG LAST! MY ARMADA WILL SQUASH YOU, YOU POMPOUS PRICKLY PIG!
SLOBBER, DROOL! I'M AS STOKED AS A KID ON CHRISTMAS EVE!
HNEH! HNEH!

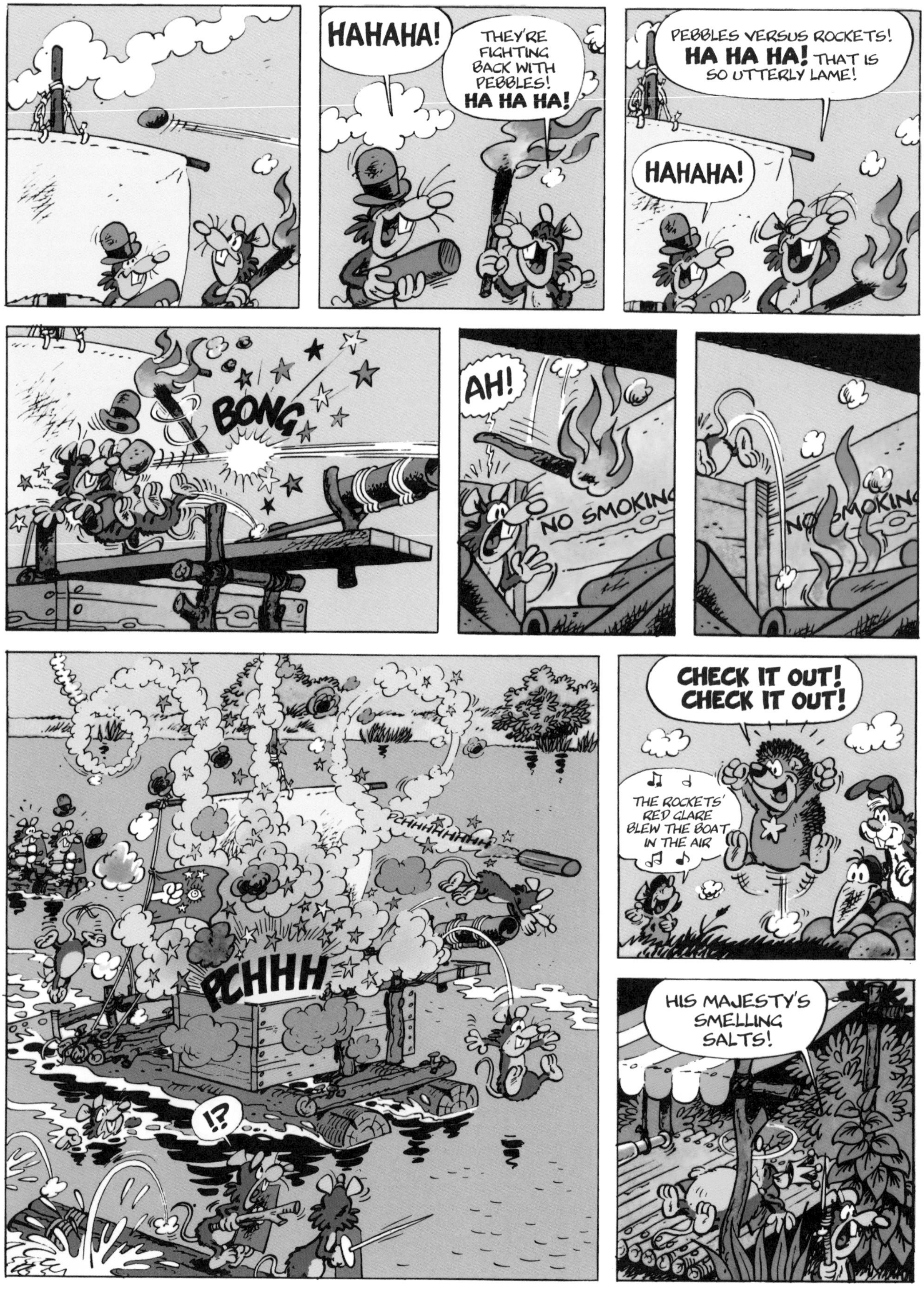
HAHAHA!
THEY'RE FIGHTING BACK WITH PEBBLES! HA HA HA!
PEBBLES VERSUS ROCKETS! HA HA HA! THAT IS SO UTTERLY LAME!
HAHAHA!
BONG
AH!
NO SMOKING
NO SMOKING
PCHHHHHHHH
PCHHH
!?
CHECK IT OUT! CHECK IT OUT!
THE ROCKETS' RED GLARE BLEW THE BOAT IN THE AIR
HIS MAJESTY'S SMELLING SALTS!

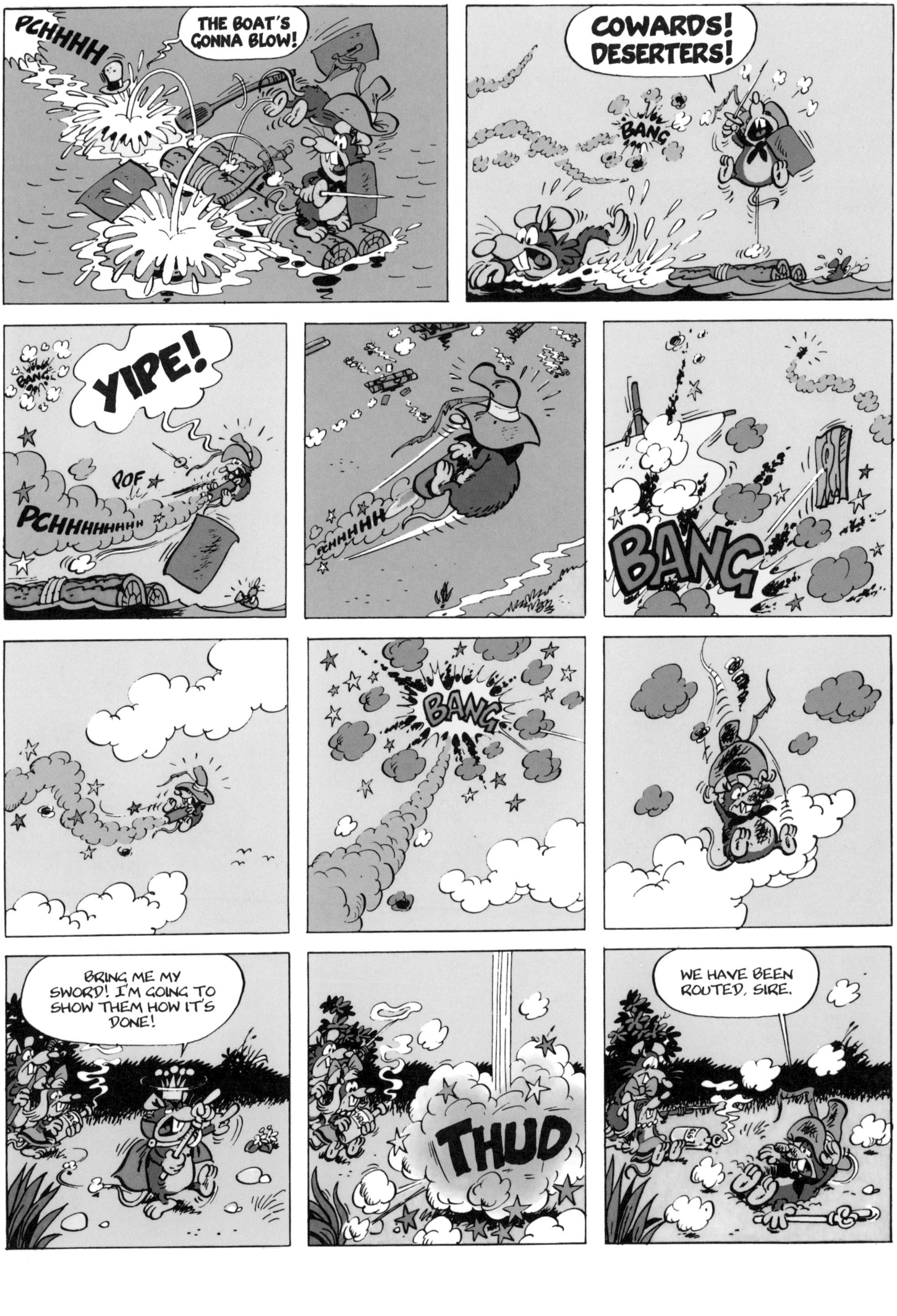
PCHHHH
THE BOAT'S GONNA BLOW!
COWARDS! DESERTERS!
BANG
YIPE!
BANG
POF
PCHHHHHHHH
PCHHHHHH
BANG
BANG
BRING ME MY SWORD! I'M GOING TO SHOW THEM HOW IT'S DONE!
THUD
WE HAVE BEEN ROUTED, SIRE.

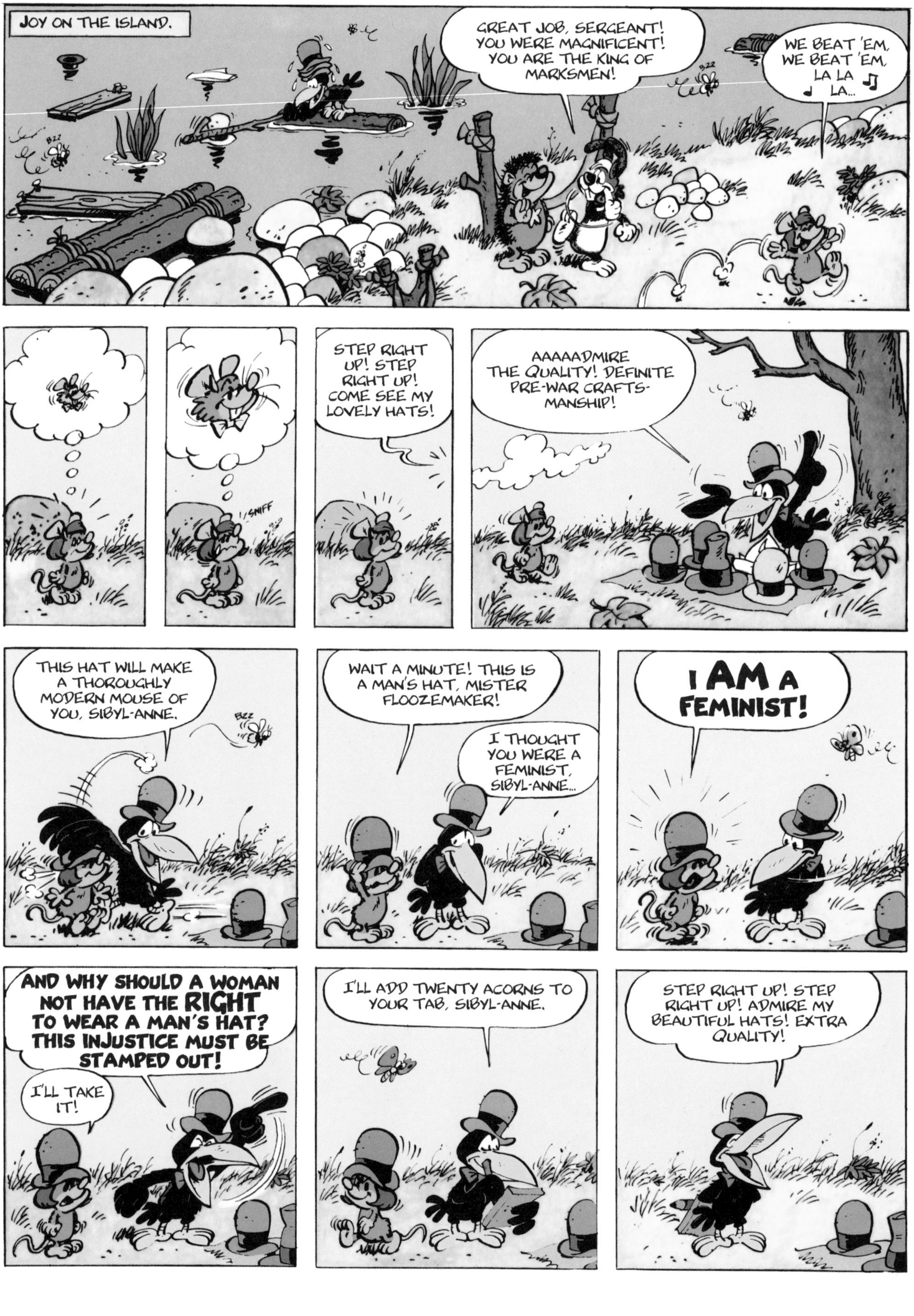

JOY ON THE ISLAND.
GREAT JOB, SERGEANT! YOU WERE MAGNIFICENT! YOU ARE THE KING OF MARKSMEN!
WE BEAT 'EM, WE BEAT 'EM, LA LA LA...
BZZ
SNIFF
STEP RIGHT UP! STEP RIGHT UP! COME SEE MY LOVELY HATS!
AAAAADMIRE THE QUALITY! DEFINITE PRE-WAR CRAFTSMANSHIP!
THIS HAT WILL MAKE A THOROUGHLY MODERN MOUSE OF YOU, SIBYL-ANNE.
BZZ
WAIT A MINUTE! THIS IS A MAN'S HAT, MISTER FLOOZEMAKER!
I THOUGHT YOU WERE A FEMINIST, SIBYL-ANNE...
I AM A FEMINIST!
AND WHY SHOULD A WOMAN NOT HAVE THE RIGHT TO WEAR A MAN'S HAT? THIS INJUSTICE MUST BE STAMPED OUT!
I'LL TAKE IT!
I'LL ADD TWENTY ACORNS TO YOUR TAB, SIBYL-ANNE.
STEP RIGHT UP! STEP RIGHT UP! ADMIRE MY BEAUTIFUL HATS! EXTRA QUALITY!

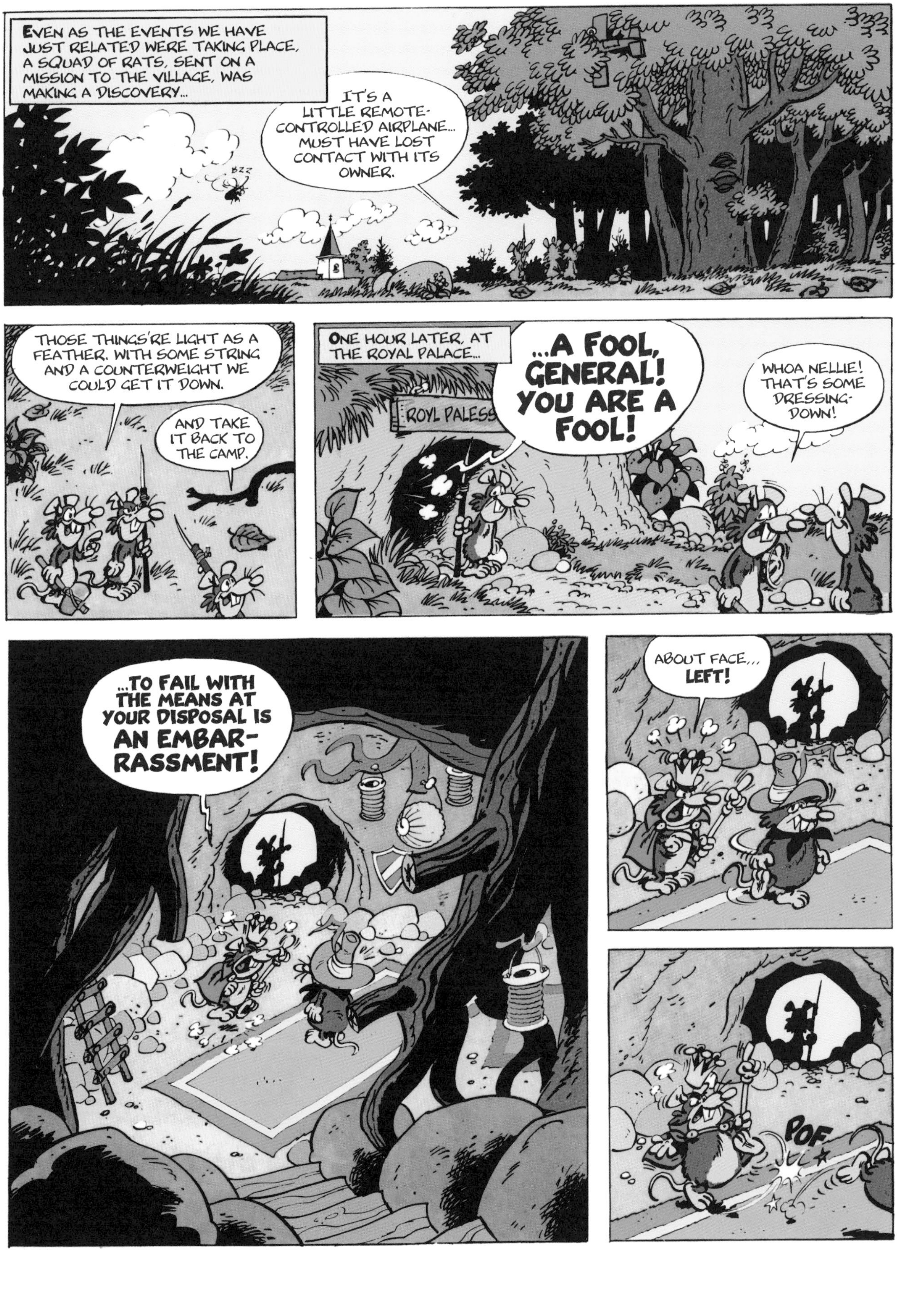
EVEN AS THE EVENTS WE HAVE JUST RELATED WERE TAKING PLACE, A SQUAD OF RATS, SENT ON A MISSION TO THE VILLAGE, WAS MAKING A DISCOVERY...
BZZ
IT'S A LITTLE REMOTE-CONTROLLED AIRPLANE... MUST HAVE LOST CONTACT WITH ITS OWNER.
THOSE THINGS'RE LIGHT AS A FEATHER. WITH SOME STRING AND A COUNTERWEIGHT WE COULD GET IT DOWN.
AND TAKE IT BACK TO THE CAMP.
ONE HOUR LATER, AT THE ROYAL PALACE...
ROYL PALESS
...A FOOL, GENERAL! YOU ARE A FOOL!
WHOA NELLIE! THAT'S SOME DRESSING-DOWN!
...TO FAIL WITH THE MEANS AT YOUR DISPOSAL IS AN EMBARRASSMENT!
ABOUT FACE,,, LEFT!
POF

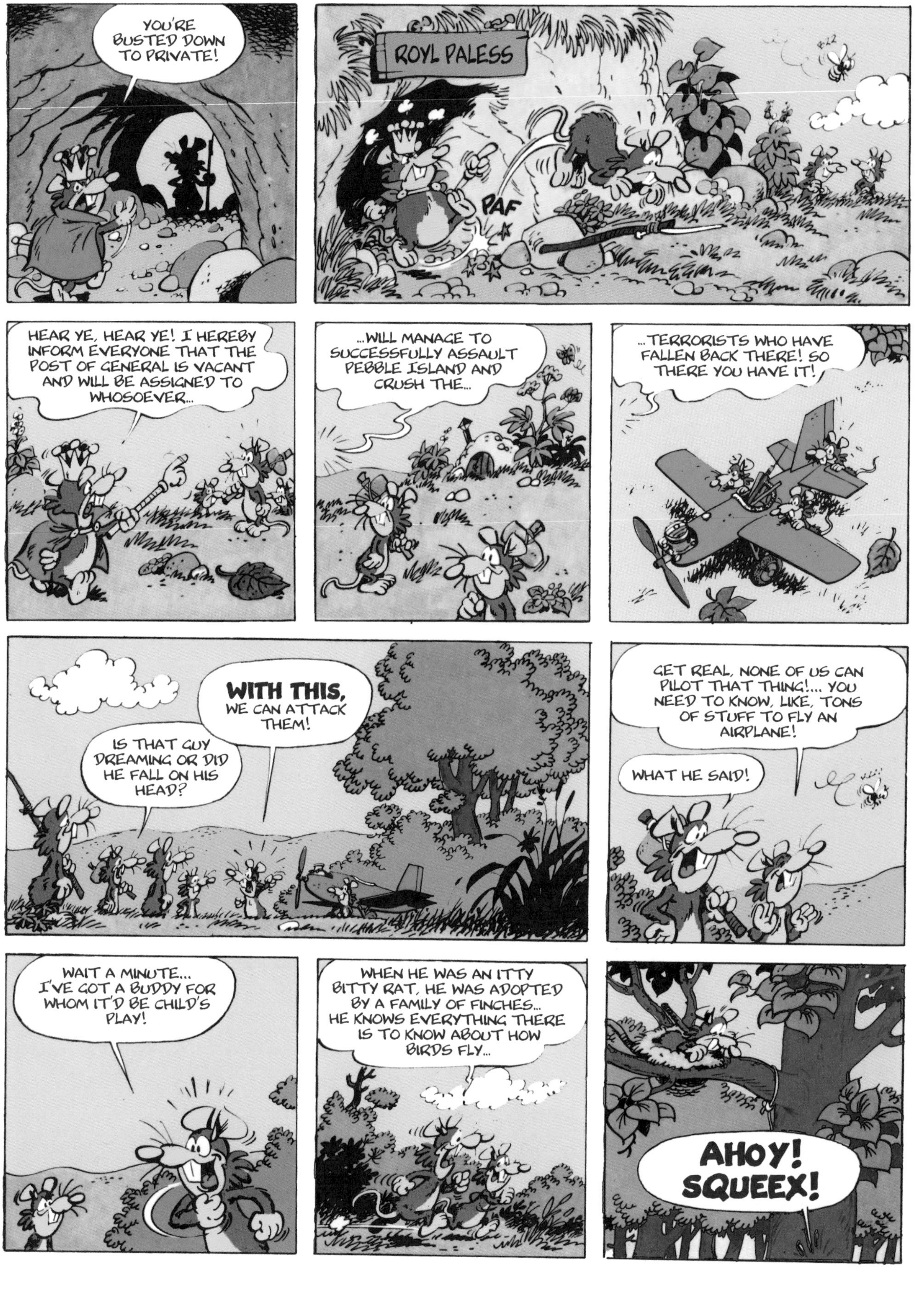
YOU'RE BUSTED DOWN TO PRIVATE!
ROYL PALESS
BZZ
PAF
HEAR YE, HEAR YE! I HEREBY INFORM EVERYONE THAT THE POST OF GENERAL IS VACANT AND WILL BE ASSIGNED TO WHOSOEVER...
...WILL MANAGE TO SUCCESSFULLY ASSAULT PEBBLE ISLAND AND CRUSH THE...
...TERRORISTS WHO HAVE FALLEN BACK THERE! SO THERE YOU HAVE IT!
WITH THIS, WE CAN ATTACK THEM!
IS THAT GUY DREAMING OR DID HE FALL ON HIS HEAD?
GET REAL, NONE OF US CAN PILOT THAT THING!... YOU NEED TO KNOW, LIKE, TONS OF STUFF TO FLY AN AIRPLANE!
WHAT HE SAID!
WAIT A MINUTE... I'VE GOT A BUDDY FOR WHOM IT'D BE CHILD'S PLAY!
WHEN HE WAS AN ITTY BITTY RAT, HE WAS ADOPTED BY A FAMILY OF FINCHES... HE KNOWS EVERYTHING THERE IS TO KNOW ABOUT HOW BIRDS FLY...
AHOY! SQUEEX!

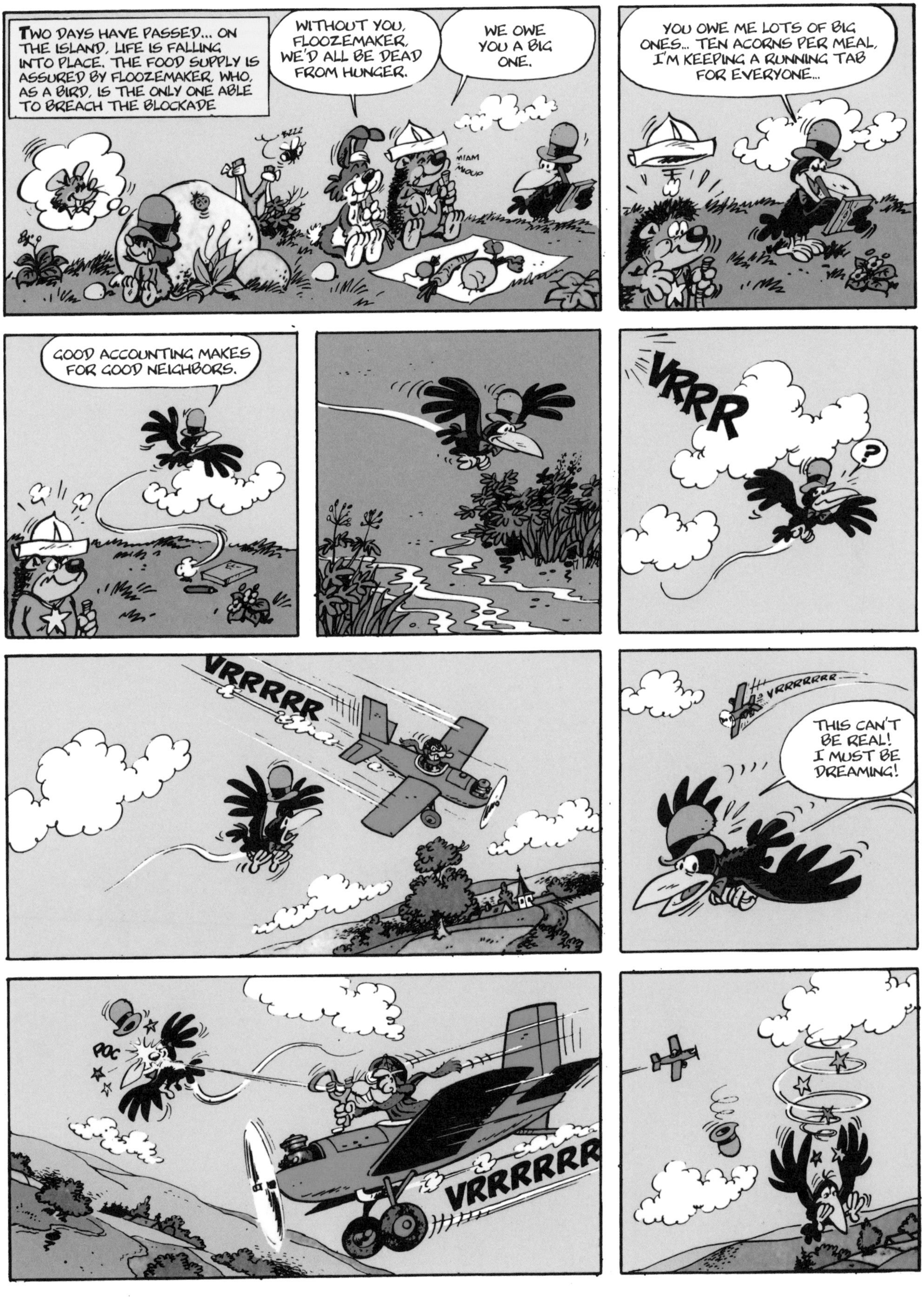
TWO DAYS HAVE PASSED... ON THE ISLAND, LIFE IS FALLING INTO PLACE. THE FOOD SUPPLY IS ASSURED BY FLOOZEMAKER, WHO, AS A BIRD, IS THE ONLY ONE ABLE TO BREACH THE BLOCKADE
WITHOUT YOU, FLOOZEMAKER, WE'D ALL BE DEAD FROM HUNGER.
WE OWE YOU A BIG ONE.
BZZZ
MIAM
MIOUP
YOU OWE ME LOTS OF BIG ONES... TEN ACORNS PER MEAL, I'M KEEPING A RUNNING TAB FOR EVERYONE...
GOOD ACCOUNTING MAKES FOR GOOD NEIGHBORS.
VRRR
?
VRRRRRR
VRRRRRRR
THIS CAN'T BE REAL! I MUST BE DREAMING!
POC
VRRRRRR

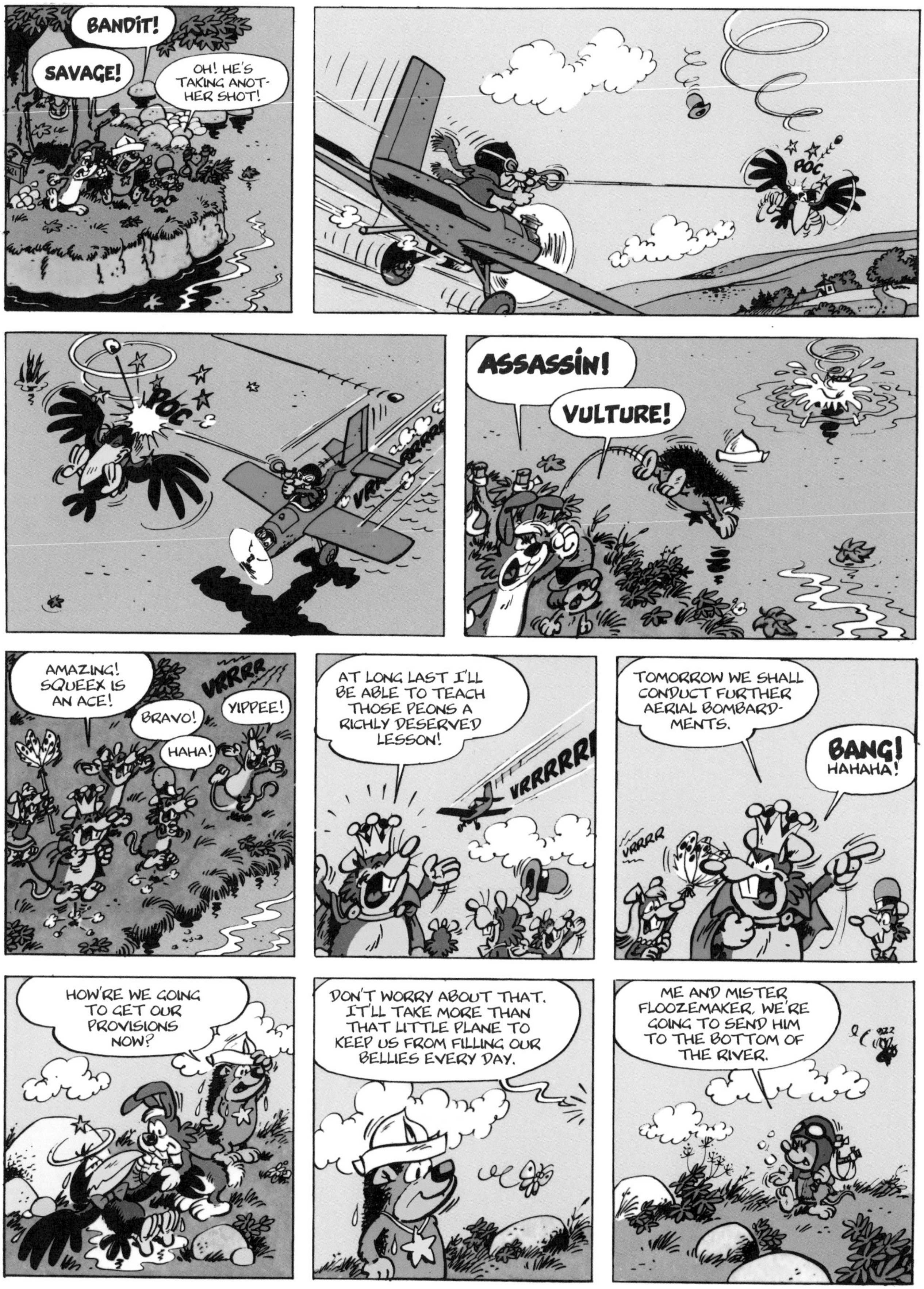
BANDIT!
SAVAGE!
OH! HE'S TAKING ANOTHER SHOT!
POC
POC
VRRRRRR
ASSASSIN!
VULTURE!
AMAZING! SQUEEX IS AN ACE!
VRRRR
BRAVO!
YIPPEE!
HAHA!
AT LONG LAST I'LL BE ABLE TO TEACH THOSE PEONS A RICHLY DESERVED LESSON!
VRRRRRR
TOMORROW WE SHALL CONDUCT FURTHER AERIAL BOMBARDMENTS.
BANG! HAHAHA!
VRRRR
HOW'RE WE GOING TO GET OUR PROVISIONS NOW?
DON'T WORRY ABOUT THAT. IT'LL TAKE MORE THAN THAT LITTLE PLANE TO KEEP US FROM FILLING OUR BELLIES EVERY DAY.
ME AND MISTER FLOOZEMAKER, WE'RE GOING TO SEND HIM TO THE BOTTOM OF THE RIVER.

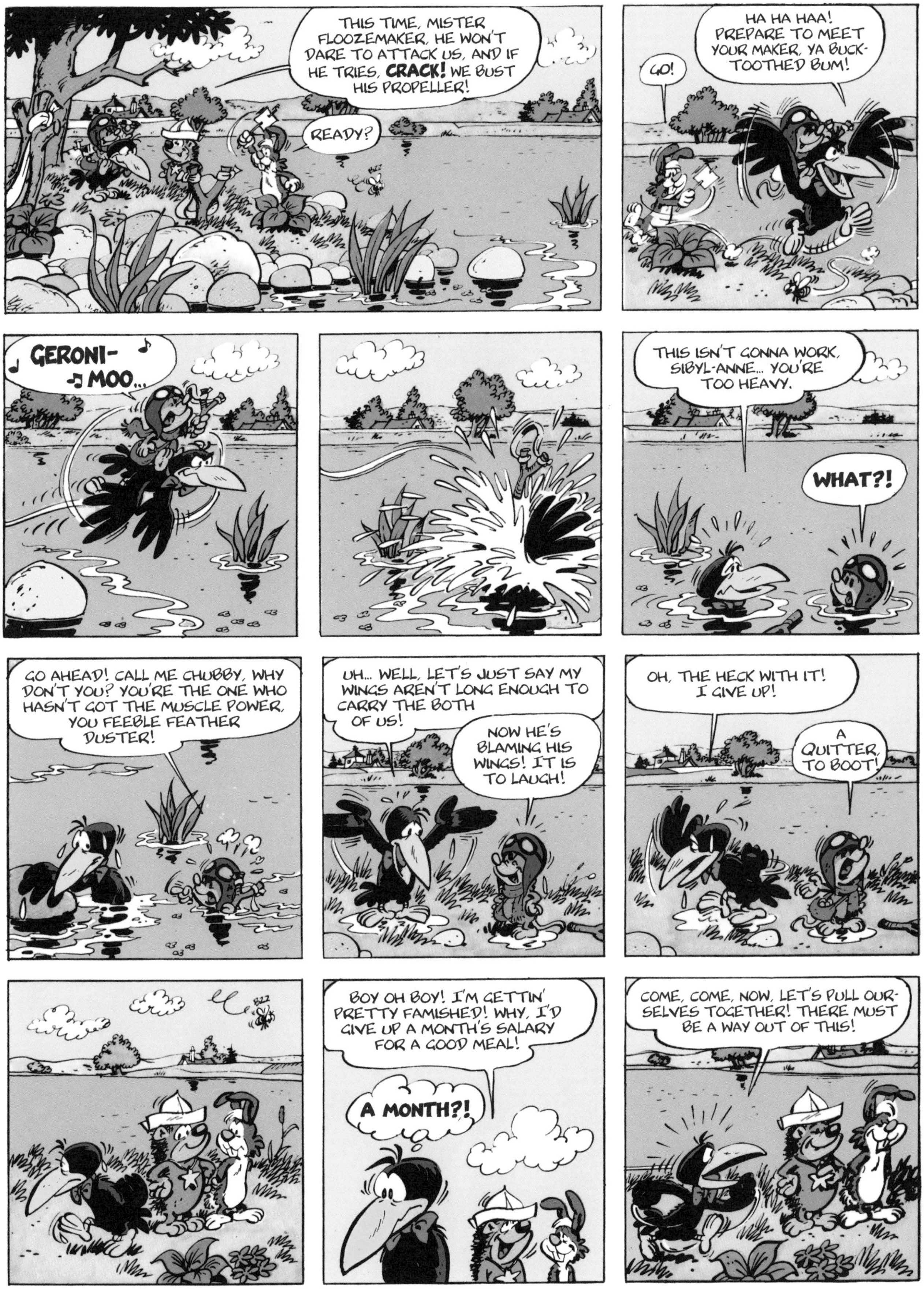
THIS TIME, MISTER FLOOZEMAKER, HE WON'T DARE TO ATTACK US, AND IF HE TRIES, **CRACK!** WE BUST HIS PROPELLER!
READY?
HA HA HAA! PREPARE TO MEET YOUR MAKER, YA BUCK-TOOTHED BUM!
GO!
GERONI- MOO...
THIS ISN'T GONNA WORK, SIBYL-ANNE... YOU'RE TOO HEAVY.
WHAT?!
GO AHEAD! CALL ME CHUBBY, WHY DON'T YOU? YOU'RE THE ONE WHO HASN'T GOT THE MUSCLE POWER, YOU FEEBLE FEATHER DUSTER!
UH... WELL, LET'S JUST SAY MY WINGS AREN'T LONG ENOUGH TO CARRY THE BOTH OF US!
NOW HE'S BLAMING HIS WINGS! IT IS TO LAUGH!
OH, THE HECK WITH IT! I GIVE UP!
A QUITTER, TO BOOT!
BZZ
BOY OH BOY! I'M GETTIN' PRETTY FAMISHED! WHY, I'D GIVE UP A MONTH'S SALARY FOR A GOOD MEAL!
A MONTH?!
COME, COME, NOW, LET'S PULL OURSELVES TOGETHER! THERE MUST BE A WAY OUT OF THIS!

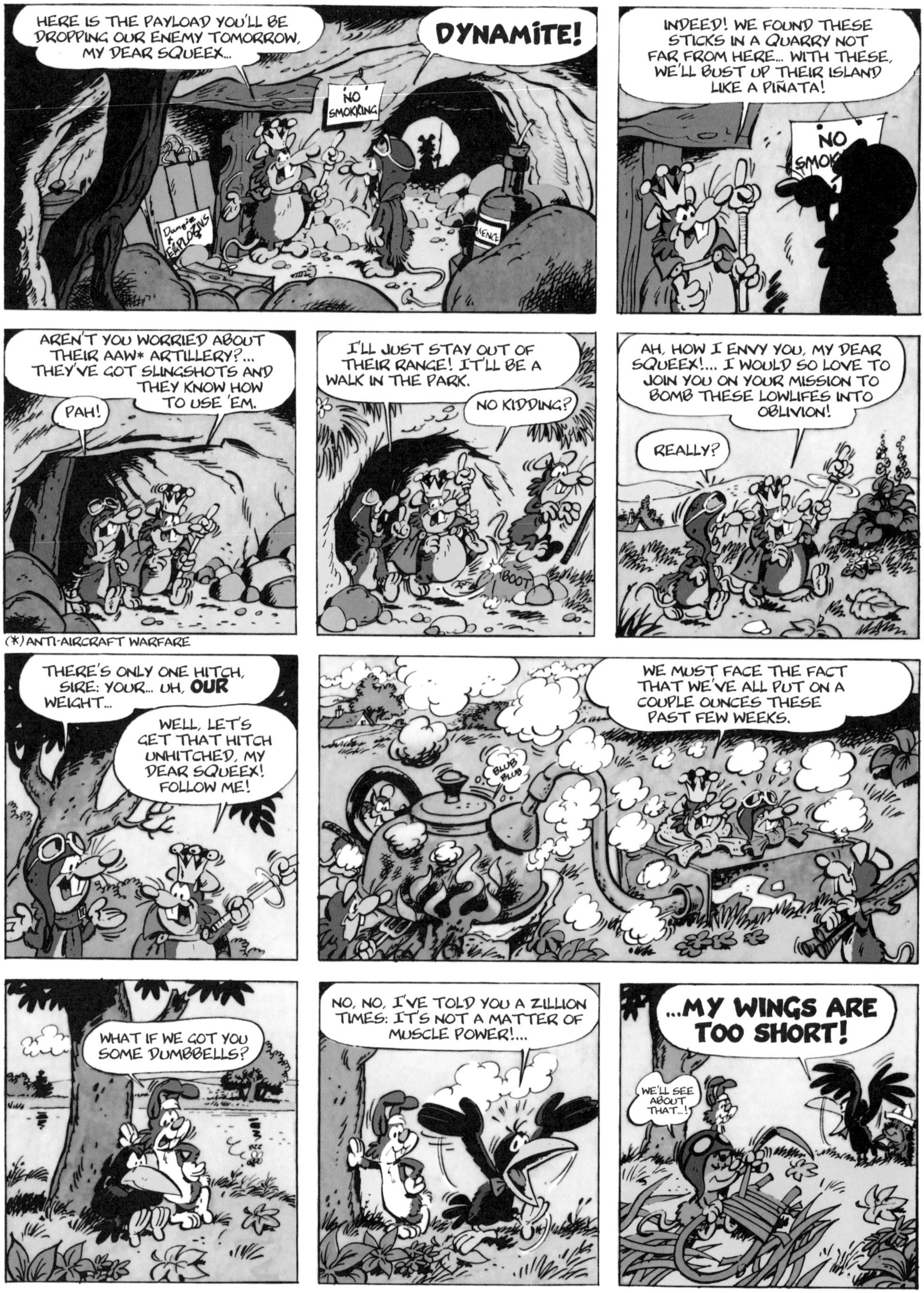
HERE IS THE PAYLOAD YOU'LL BE DROPPING OUR ENEMY TOMORROW, MY DEAR SQUEEX...
DYNAMITE!
NO SMOKING
INDEED! WE FOUND THESE STICKS IN A QUARRY NOT FAR FROM HERE... WITH THESE, WE'LL BUST UP THEIR ISLAND LIKE A PIÑATA!
NO SMOK
AREN'T YOU WORRIED ABOUT THEIR AAW* ARTILLERY?... THEY'VE GOT SLINGSHOTS AND THEY KNOW HOW TO USE 'EM.
PAH!
I'LL JUST STAY OUT OF THEIR RANGE! IT'LL BE A WALK IN THE PARK.
NO KIDDING?
BOOT
AH, HOW I ENVY YOU, MY DEAR SQUEEX!... I WOULD SO LOVE TO JOIN YOU ON YOUR MISSION TO BOMB THESE LOWLIFES INTO OBLIVION!
REALLY?
(*) ANTI-AIRCRAFT WARFARE
THERE'S ONLY ONE HITCH, SIRE: YOUR... UH, OUR WEIGHT...
WELL, LET'S GET THAT HITCH UNHITCHED, MY DEAR SQUEEX! FOLLOW ME!
WE MUST FACE THE FACT THAT WE'VE ALL PUT ON A COUPLE OUNCES THESE PAST FEW WEEKS.
BLUB BLUB
WHAT IF WE GOT YOU SOME DUMBBELLS?
NO, NO, I'VE TOLD YOU A ZILLION TIMES: IT'S NOT A MATTER OF MUSCLE POWER!...
...MY WINGS ARE TOO SHORT!
WE'LL SEE ABOUT THAT...!

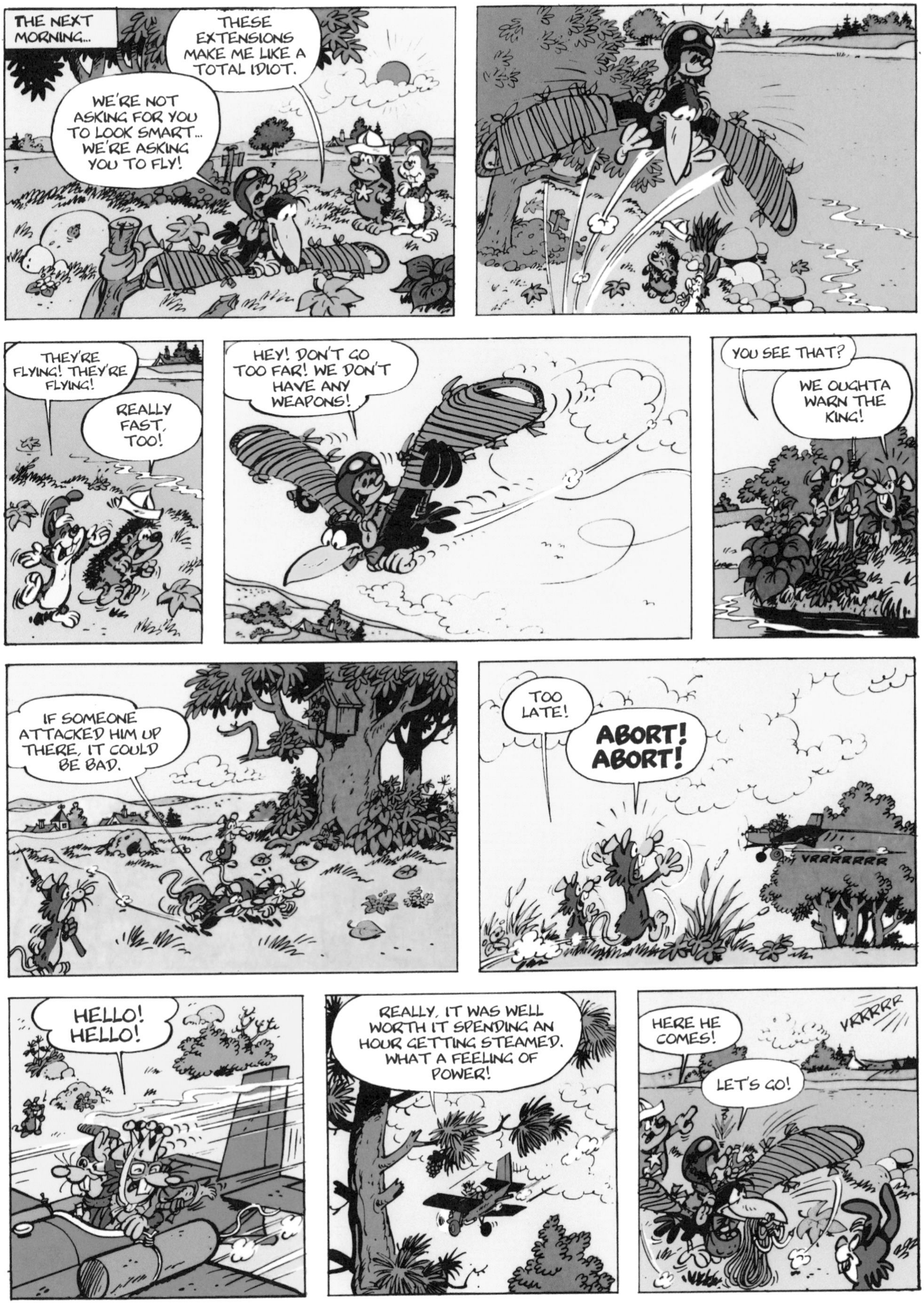
THE NEXT MORNING...
THESE EXTENSIONS MAKE ME LIKE A TOTAL IDIOT.
WE'RE NOT ASKING FOR YOU TO LOOK SMART... WE'RE ASKING YOU TO FLY!
THEY'RE FLYING! THEY'RE FLYING!
REALLY FAST, TOO!
HEY! DON'T GO TOO FAR! WE DON'T HAVE ANY WEAPONS!
YOU SEE THAT?
WE OUGHTA WARN THE KING!
IF SOMEONE ATTACKED HIM UP THERE, IT COULD BE BAD.
TOO LATE!
ABORT! ABORT!
VRRRRRRR
HELLO! HELLO!
REALLY, IT WAS WELL WORTH IT SPENDING AN HOUR GETTING STEAMED. WHAT A FEELING OF POWER!
VRRRRR
HERE HE COMES!
LET'S GO!

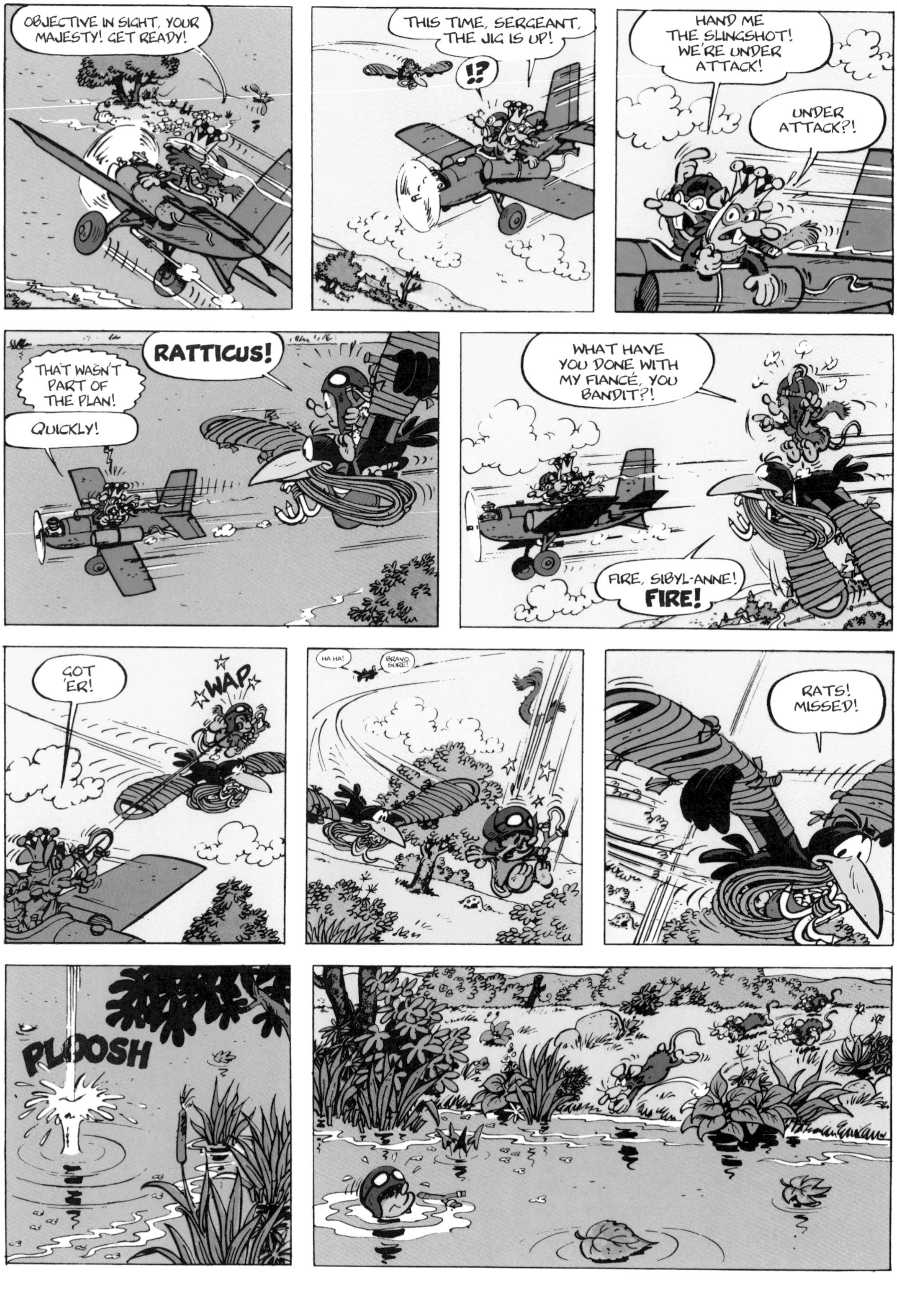
OBJECTIVE IN SIGHT, YOUR MAJESTY! GET READY!
THIS TIME, SERGEANT, THE JIG IS UP!
!?
HAND ME THE SLINGSHOT! WE'RE UNDER ATTACK!
UNDER ATTACK?!
RATTICUS!
THAT WASN'T PART OF THE PLAN!
QUICKLY!
WHAT HAVE YOU DONE WITH MY FIANCÉ, YOU BANDIT?!
FIRE, SIBYL-ANNE! FIRE!
GOT 'ER!
WAP
HA HA!
BRAVO, SURE!
RATS! MISSED!
PLOOSH

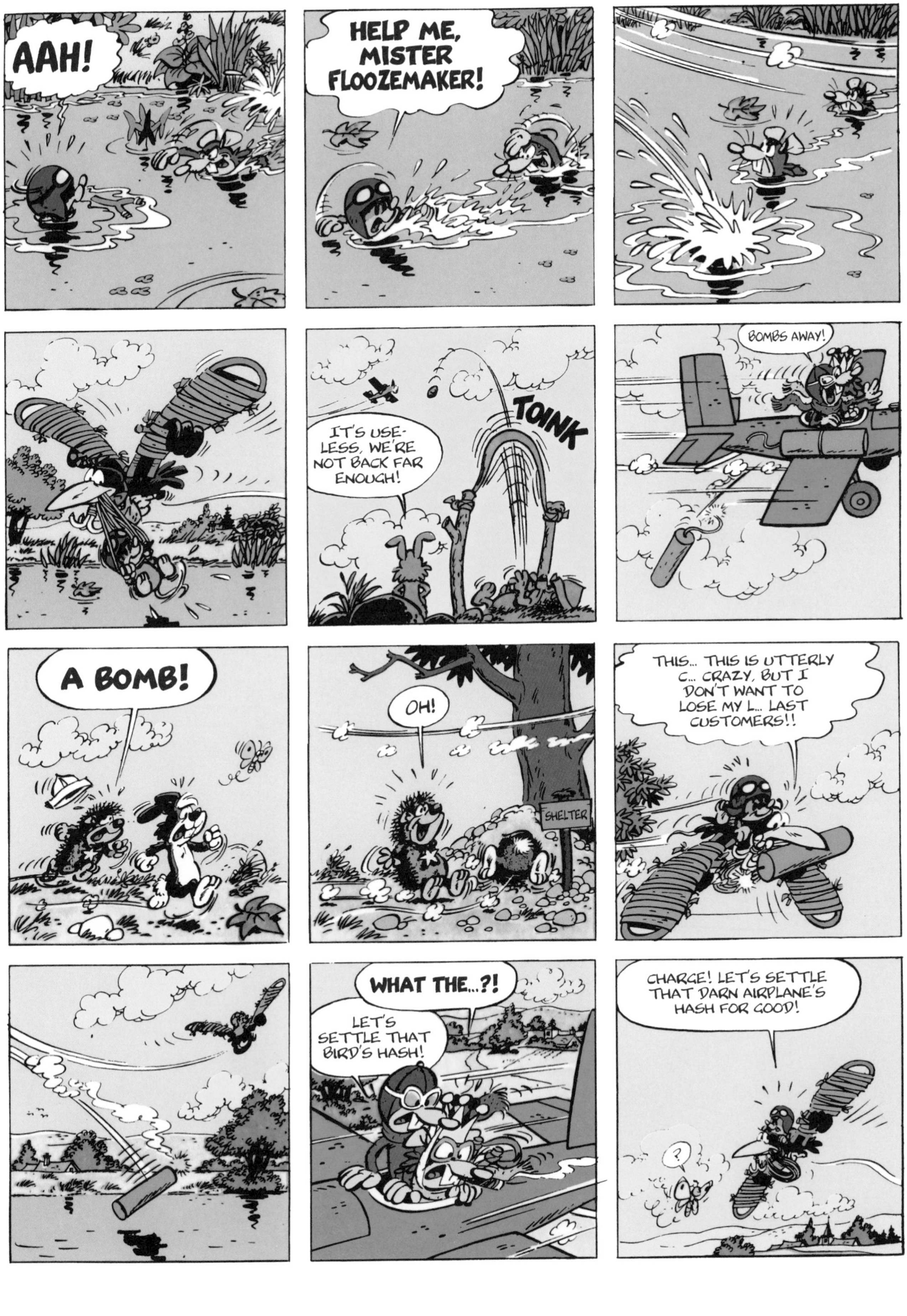
AAH!
HELP ME, MISTER FLOOZEMAKER!
IT'S USELESS, WE'RE NOT BACK FAR ENOUGH!
TOINK
BOMBS AWAY!
A BOMB!
OH!
SHELTER
THIS... THIS IS UTTERLY C... CRAZY, BUT I DON'T WANT TO LOSE MY L... LAST CUSTOMERS!!
WHAT THE...?!
LET'S SETTLE THAT BIRD'S HASH!
CHARGE! LET'S SETTLE THAT DARN AIRPLANE'S HASH FOR GOOD!
?

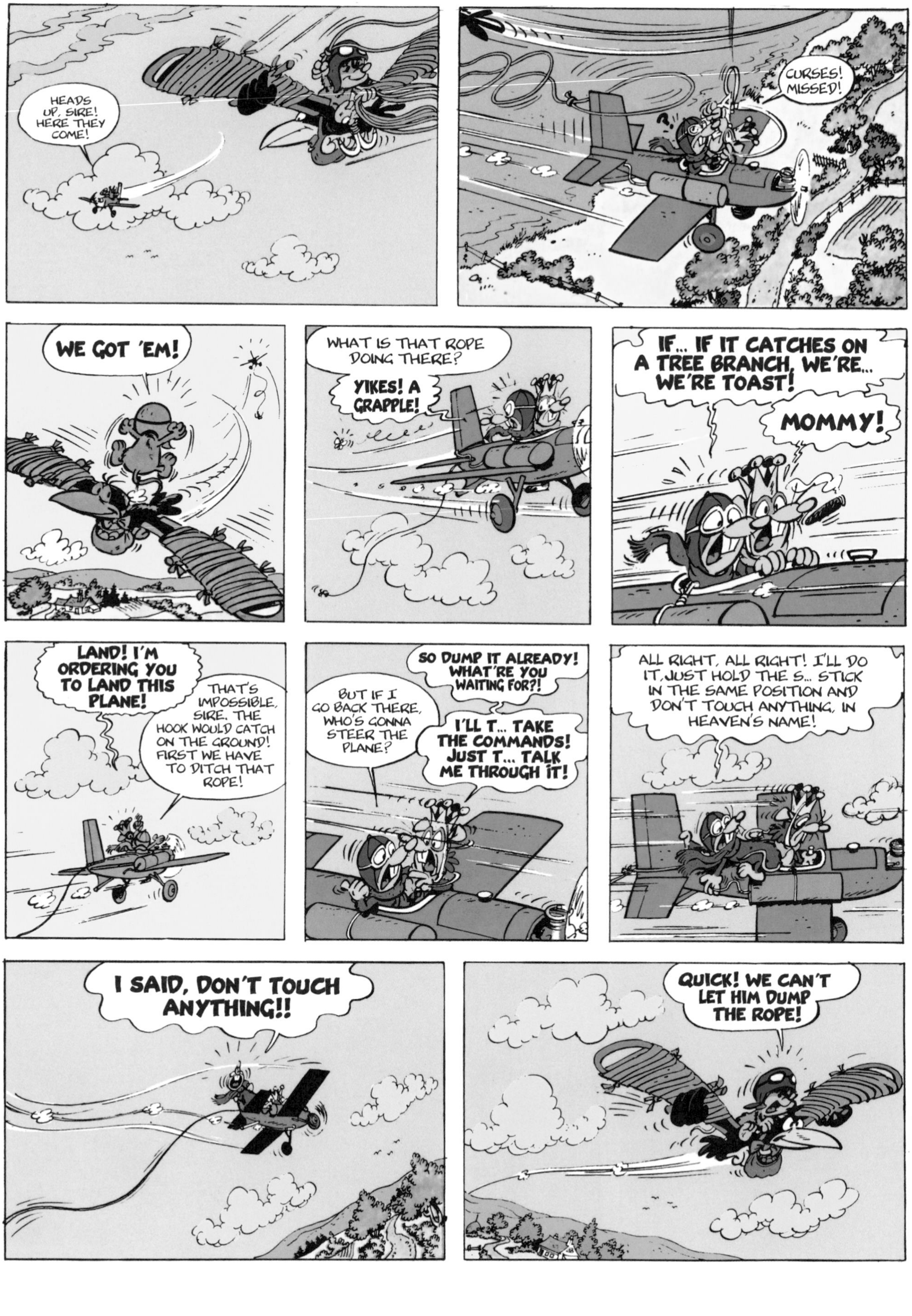
HEADS UP, SIRE! HERE THEY COME!
CURSES! MISSED!
WE GOT 'EM!
WHAT IS THAT ROPE DOING THERE?
YIKES! A GRAPPLE!
IF... IF IT CATCHES ON A TREE BRANCH, WE'RE... WE'RE TOAST!
MOMMY!
LAND! I'M ORDERING YOU TO LAND THIS PLANE!
THAT'S IMPOSSIBLE, SIRE. THE HOOK WOULD CATCH ON THE GROUND! FIRST WE HAVE TO DITCH THAT ROPE!
SO DUMP IT ALREADY! WHAT'RE YOU WAITING FOR?!
BUT IF I GO BACK THERE, WHO'S GONNA STEER THE PLANE?
I'LL T... TAKE THE COMMANDS! JUST T... TALK ME THROUGH IT!
ALL RIGHT, ALL RIGHT! I'LL DO IT, JUST HOLD THE S... STICK IN THE SAME POSITION AND DON'T TOUCH ANYTHING, IN HEAVEN'S NAME!
I SAID, DON'T TOUCH ANYTHING!!
QUICK! WE CAN'T LET HIM DUMP THE ROPE!

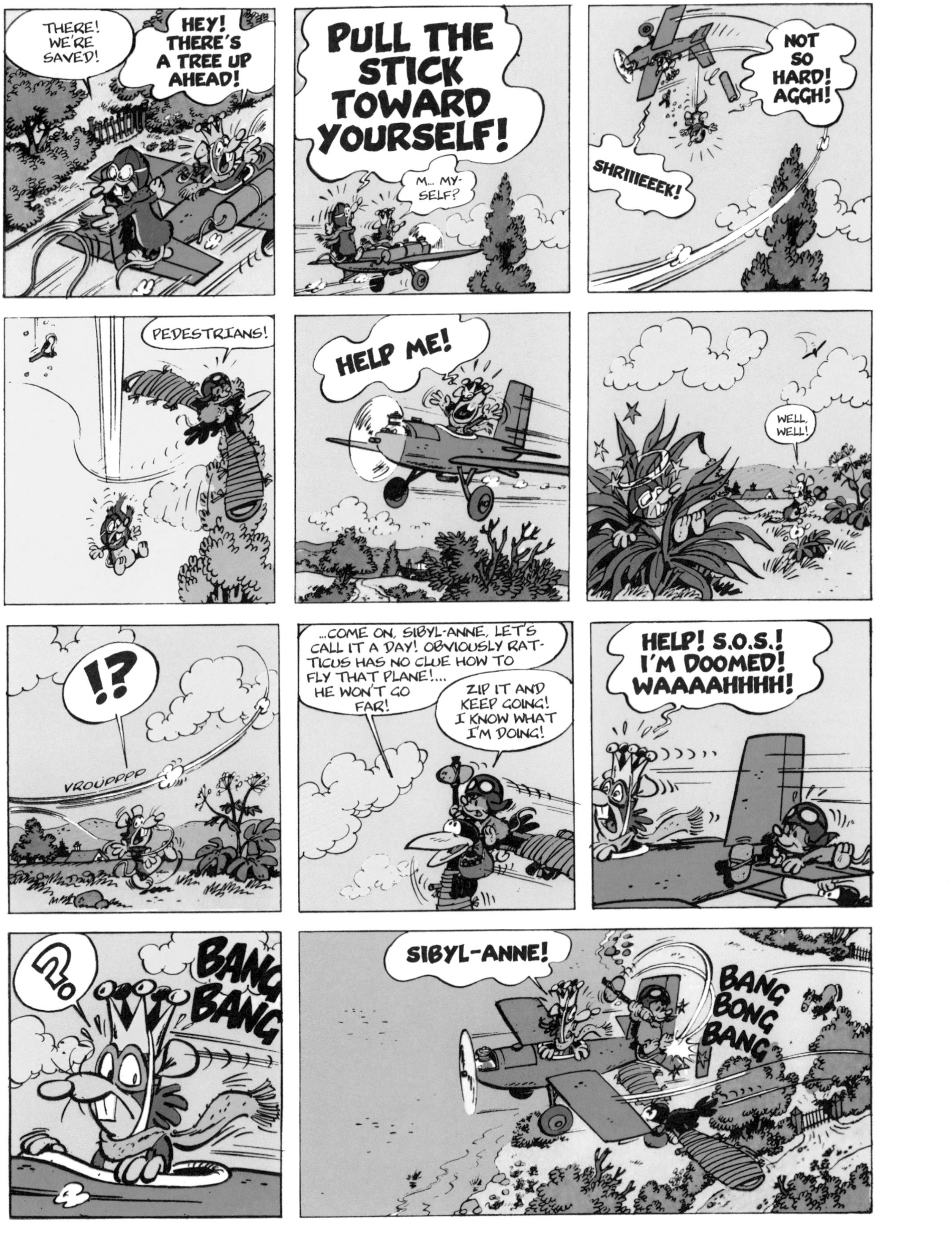
THERE! WE'RE SAVED!
HEY! THERE'S A TREE UP AHEAD!
PULL THE STICK TOWARD YOURSELF!
M... MY-SELF?
NOT SO HARD! AGGH!
SHRIIIEEEK!
PEDESTRIANS!
HELP ME!
WELL, WELL!
!?
VROUPPPP
...COME ON, SIBYL-ANNE, LET'S CALL IT A DAY! OBVIOUSLY RATTICUS HAS NO CLUE HOW TO FLY THAT PLANE!... HE WON'T GO FAR!
ZIP IT AND KEEP GOING! I KNOW WHAT I'M DOING!
HELP! S.O.S.! I'M DOOMED! WAAAAHHHH!
?
BANG BANG
SIBYL-ANNE!
BANG BONG BANG

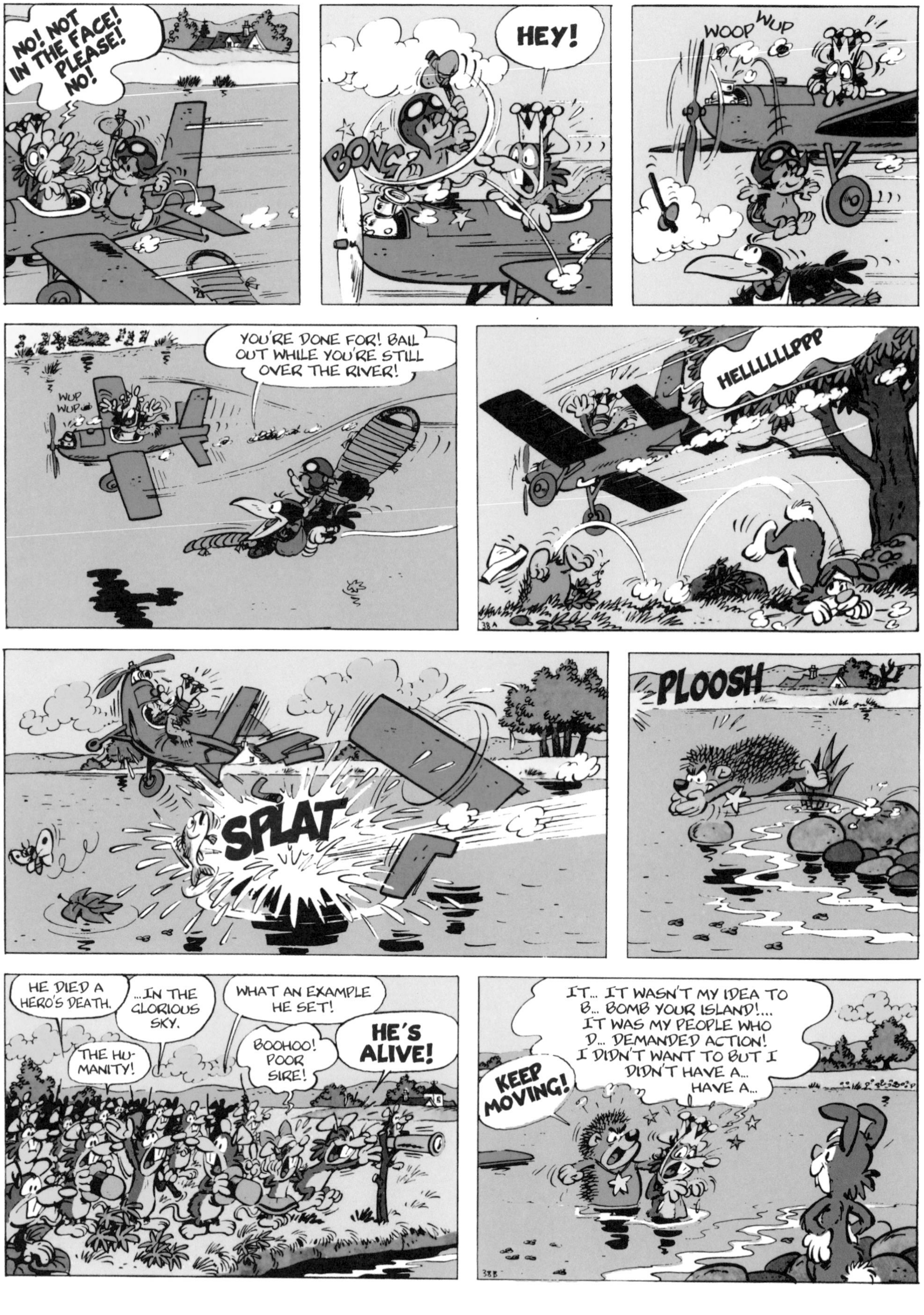
NO! NOT IN THE FACE! PLEASE! NO!
BONG
HEY!
WOOP WUP
YOU'RE DONE FOR! BAIL OUT WHILE YOU'RE STILL OVER THE RIVER!
WUP WUP
HELLLLLLPPP
SPLAT
PLOOSH
HE DIED A HERO'S DEATH.
...IN THE GLORIOUS SKY.
THE HU-MANITY!
WHAT AN EXAMPLE HE SET!
BOOHOO! POOR SIRE!
HE'S ALIVE!
IT... IT WASN'T MY IDEA TO B... BOMB YOUR ISLAND!.... IT WAS MY PEOPLE WHO D... DEMANDED ACTION! I DIDN'T WANT TO BUT I DIDN'T HAVE A... HAVE A...
KEEP MOVING!

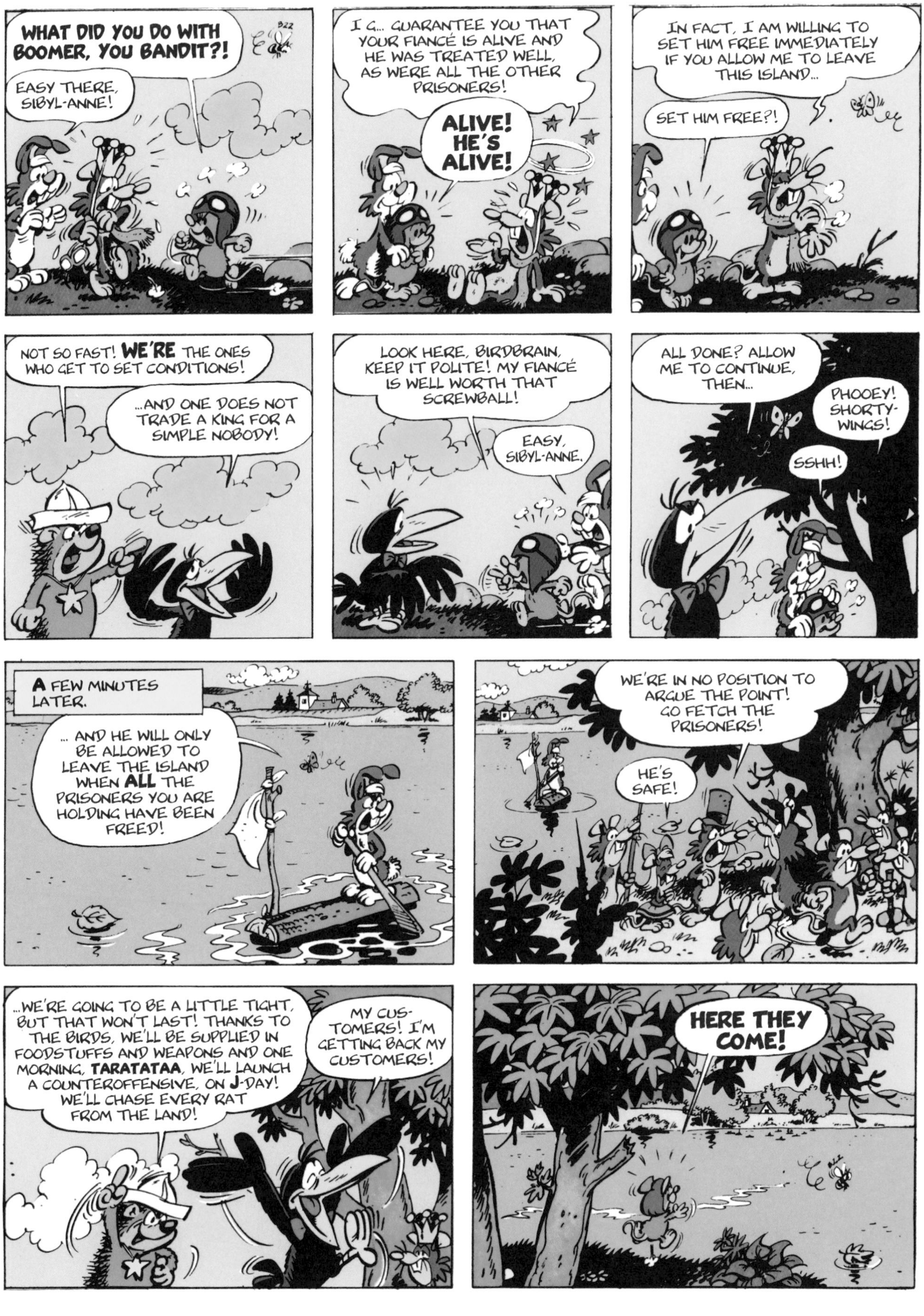
WHAT DID YOU DO WITH BOOMER, YOU BANDIT?!
EASY THERE, SIBYL-ANNE!
BZZ
I G... GUARANTEE YOU THAT YOUR FIANCÉ IS ALIVE AND HE WAS TREATED WELL, AS WERE ALL THE OTHER PRISONERS!
ALIVE! HE'S ALIVE!
IN FACT, I AM WILLING TO SET HIM FREE IMMEDIATELY IF YOU ALLOW ME TO LEAVE THIS ISLAND...
SET HIM FREE?!
NOT SO FAST! WE'RE THE ONES WHO GET TO SET CONDITIONS!
...AND ONE DOES NOT TRADE A KING FOR A SIMPLE NOBODY!
LOOK HERE, BIRDBRAIN, KEEP IT POLITE! MY FIANCÉ IS WELL WORTH THAT SCREWBALL!
EASY, SIBYL-ANNE.
ALL DONE? ALLOW ME TO CONTINUE, THEN...
PHOOEY! SHORTY-WINGS!
SSHH!
A FEW MINUTES LATER.
... AND HE WILL ONLY BE ALLOWED TO LEAVE THE ISLAND WHEN ALL THE PRISONERS YOU ARE HOLDING HAVE BEEN FREED!
WE'RE IN NO POSITION TO ARGUE THE POINT! GO FETCH THE PRISONERS!
HE'S SAFE!
...WE'RE GOING TO BE A LITTLE TIGHT, BUT THAT WON'T LAST! THANKS TO THE BIRDS, WE'LL BE SUPPLIED IN FOODSTUFFS AND WEAPONS AND ONE MORNING, TARATATAA, WE'LL LAUNCH A COUNTEROFFENSIVE, ON J-DAY! WE'LL CHASE EVERY RAT FROM THE LAND!
MY CUS-TOMERS! I'M GETTING BACK MY CUSTOMERS!
HERE THEY COME!

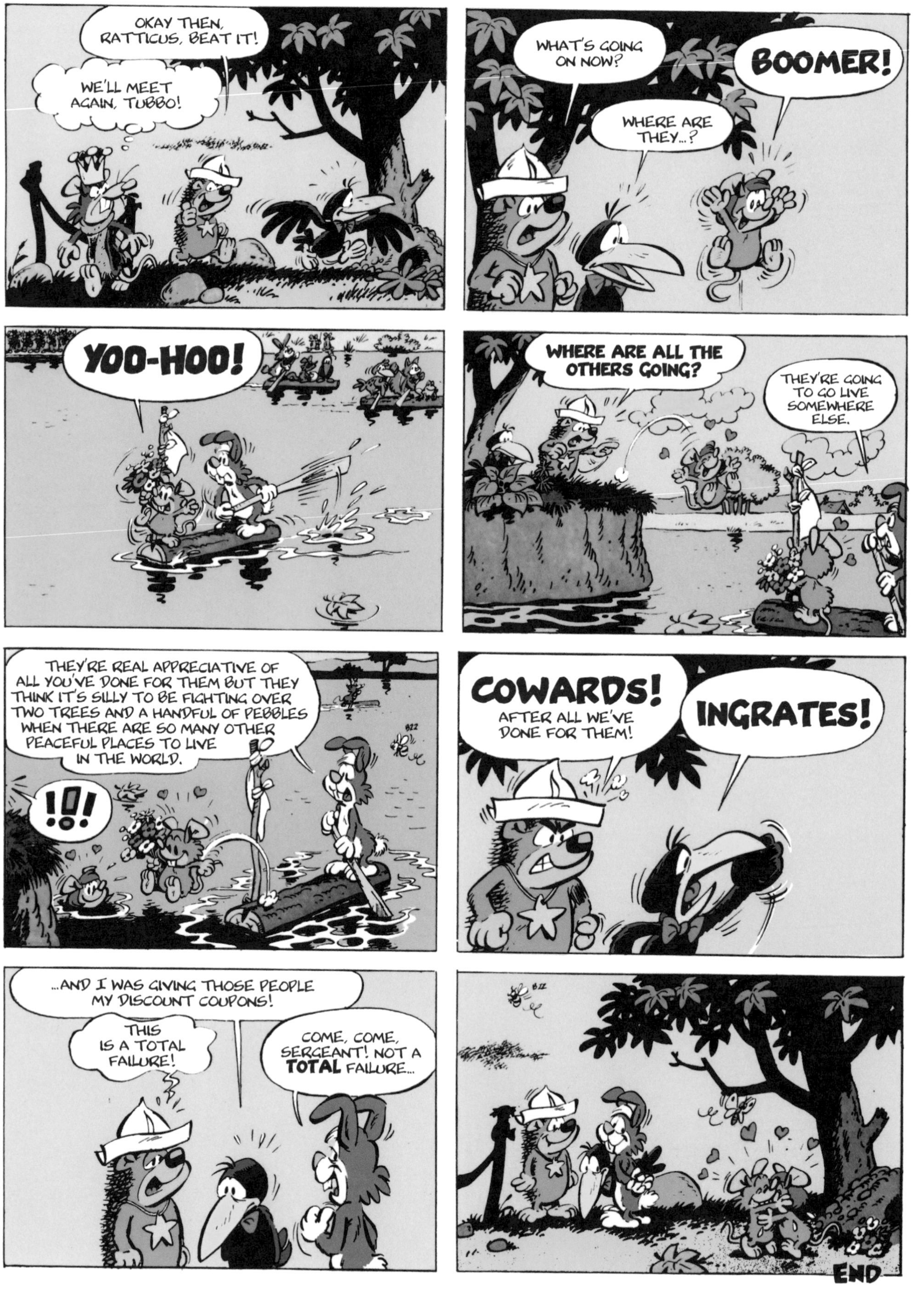
OKAY THEN, RATTICUS, BEAT IT!
WE'LL MEET AGAIN, TUBBO!
WHAT'S GOING ON NOW?
WHERE ARE THEY...?
BOOMER!
YOO-HOO!
WHERE ARE ALL THE OTHERS GOING?
THEY'RE GOING TO GO LIVE SOMEWHERE ELSE.
THEY'RE REAL APPRECIATIVE OF ALL YOU'VE DONE FOR THEM BUT THEY THINK IT'S SILLY TO BE FIGHTING OVER TWO TREES AND A HANDFUL OF PEBBLES WHEN THERE ARE SO MANY OTHER PEACEFUL PLACES TO LIVE IN THE WORLD.
!?!
BZZ
COWARDS! AFTER ALL WE'VE DONE FOR THEM!
INGRATES!
...AND I WAS GIVING THOSE PEOPLE MY DISCOUNT COUPONS!
THIS IS A TOTAL FAILURE!
COME, COME, SERGEANT! NOT A TOTAL FAILURE...
BZZ
END

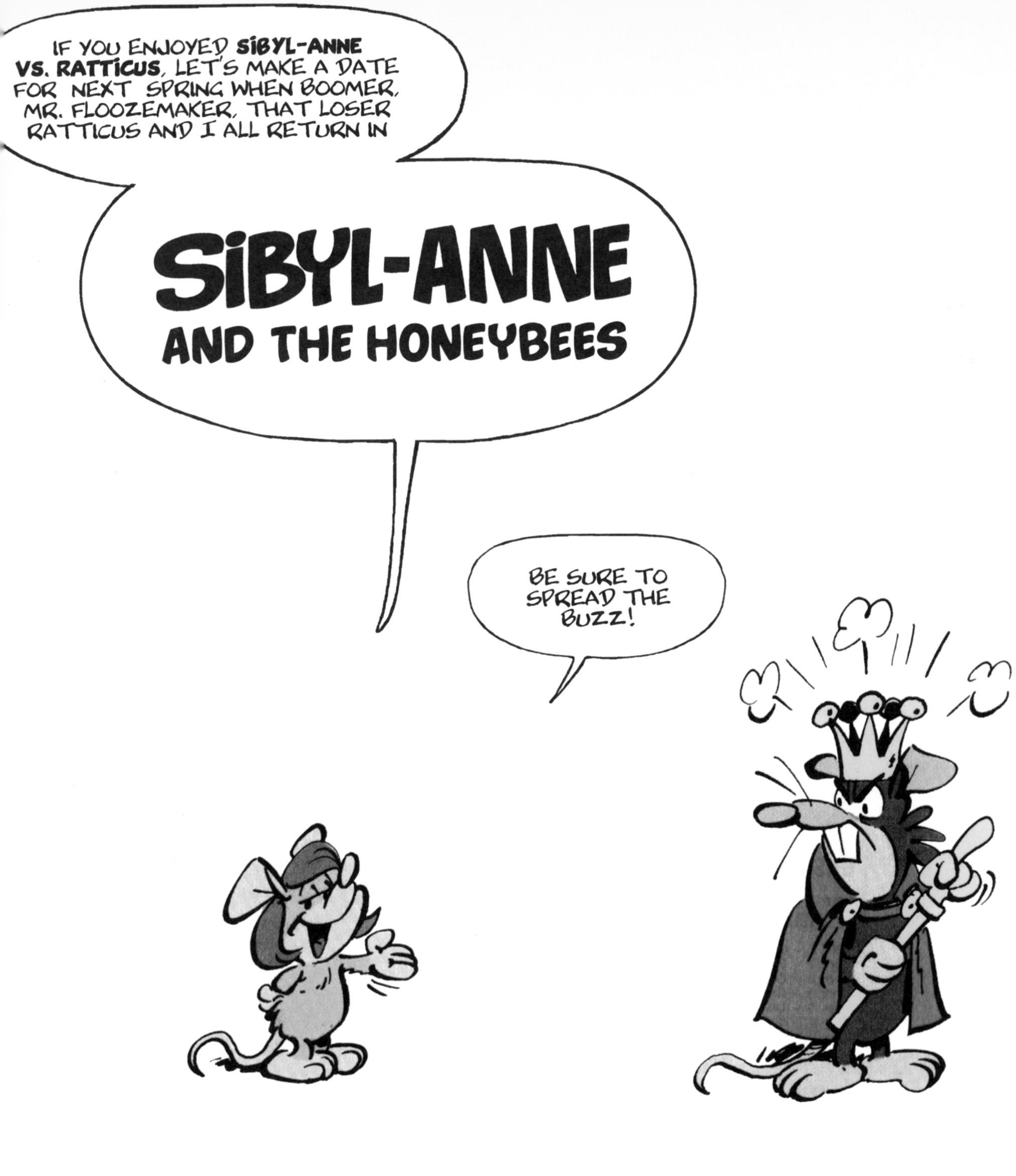
IF YOU ENJOYED SIBYL-ANNE VS. RATTICUS, LET'S MAKE A DATE FOR NEXT SPRING WHEN BOOMER, MR. FLOOZEMAKER, THAT LOSER RATTICUS AND I ALL RETURN IN
SIBYL-ANNE AND THE HONEYBEES
BE SURE TO SPREAD THE BUZZ!

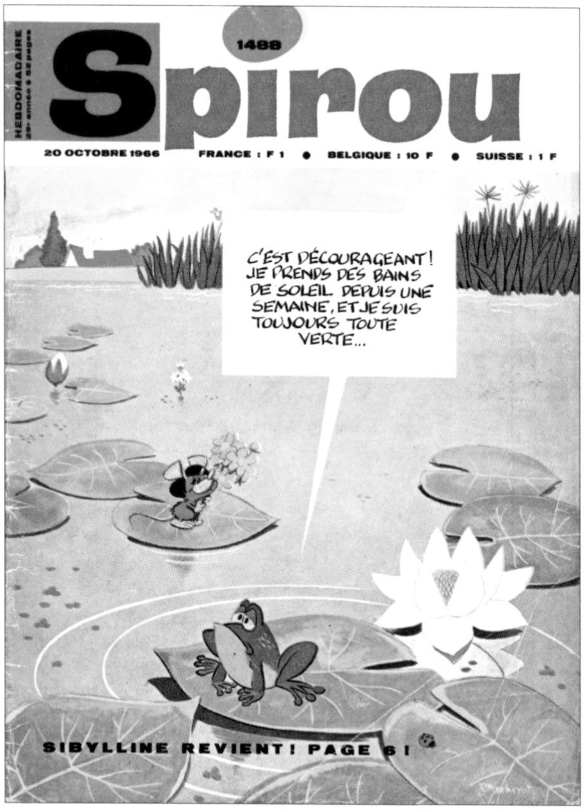
HEBDOMADAIRE
1488
Spirou
20 OCTOBRE 1966
FRANCE : F 1 ● BELGIQUE : 10 F ● SUISSE : 1 F
C'EST DÉCOURAGEANT! JE PRENDS DES BAINS DE SOLEIL DEPUIS UNE SEMAINE, ET JE SUIS TOUJOURS TOUTE VERTE...
SIBYLLINE REVIENT! PAGE 6!

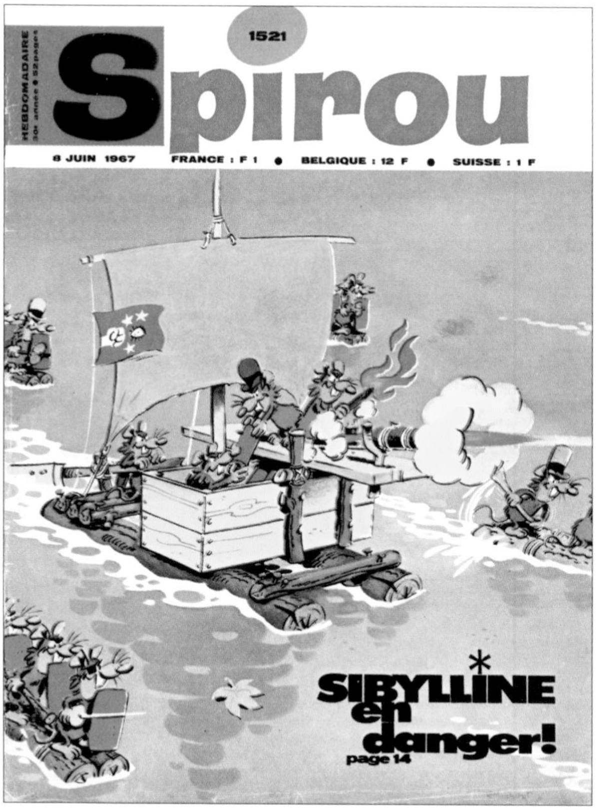
HEBDOMADAIRE
1521
Spirou
8 JUIN 1967
FRANCE : F 1 ● BELGIQUE : 12 F ● SUISSE : 1 F
SIBYLLINE en danger!
page 14

The adventures of Sibyl-Anne were originally serialized in *Spirou* magazine. Here are the two covers she graced as the stories included in *Sibyl-Anne Vs. Ratticus* ran in *Spirou*. In the first one — a gag which is not related to the story, but heralded Sibyl-Anne's return to the magazine — the frog is complaining, "It's discouraging! I've been taking sun baths for a week now, and I'm still completely green..." The second one illustrates the lead-up to the climactic battle that occurs toward the end of the book.

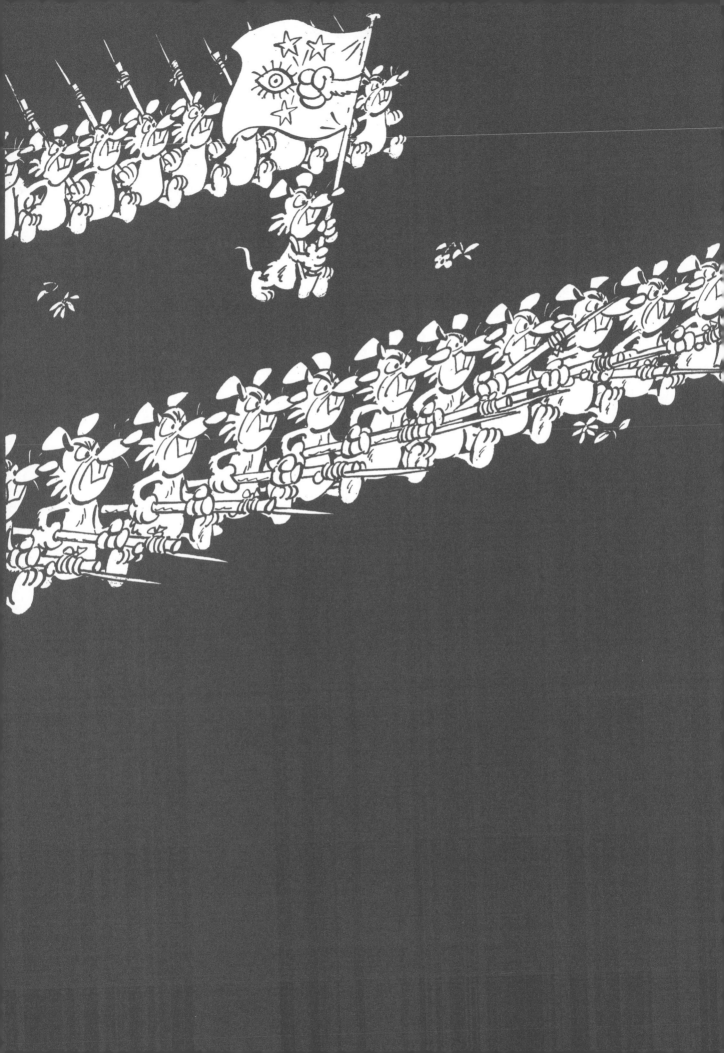